A Young African ... Assistant Football Coach Finds Himself In The Middle Of A National Recruiting War Over His Star Player

"This is a very quaint, and very real, depiction of how a small town in the South can suddenly take on a whole different feel when a player on its football team is labeled as a major prospect."—***Pete Yanity, Sports journalist for WSPA TV Spartanburg, SC/ Former play-by-play announcer for Clemson University:***

"Talented author W. Scott Jones has written a compelling and heartfelt novel with believable characters facing tough situations on and off the football field. You don't have to be a football fanatic to enjoy this story."— ***Helen Bradley, Author of Breach of Trust***

"NIL Collectives are essentially legalized (and far more lucrative) versions of the old 'hundred-dollar handshake' similar to what Author W. Scott Jones referenced in his novel. But with the same goal in mind- an overt attempt by deep-pocketed alumni to buy their alma mater a national championship."— ***Bill Contz, Author of "When the Lions Roared: Joe Paterno and One of College Football's Greatest Teams"—Former NFL player and starter on Penn State's 1982 National Championship Team:***

"As a prep sports writer for 35 years, I feel that author W. Scott Jones' depictions of coaches, players, and fans in rural areas of the Lowcountry in South Carolina are spot on accurate. What a Crowd is a great read and it brought back many great memories for me."— ***David Shelton, Sports journalist for the Charleston Post and Courier and Charleston Southern University Athletics.***

"I found What a Crowd to be an entertaining and pleasurable reading journey. Top notch reading entertainment."— ***W. P.***

Beckham, E.D.S. Author of Family History in the Great Depression:

"I am confident that countless individuals will benefit from reading this book of inspiration."— ***Christopher Mazyck, Former player at Penn State University (1994), Prevention Specialist:***

"In a time when we emphasize the outward- What a Crowd tells the story of looking inward of others and ourselves. Author W. Scott Jones beautifully weaves the religion of football in the South along with the tensions, turmoil, beauty, and all that comes with it. Enjoy this journey of football and life."— ***Mike Jones, Former player at the University of South Carolina (1999), Award winning coach and sales professional***

"Having been a high school football coach for 38 years, I love this book. It really touches on what recruiting and playing college football was like in that era. It also touches on how coaching as a profession is a calling."—***Don Frost, Four-time State Championship and South Carolina Coaches Association Hall of Fame Coach- Christ Church Episcopal School, Greenville, SC***

"This novel paints the perfect picture of how an entire town can be impacted when its high school has a major prospect."— ***Scott Earley, Executive Director of the South Carolina Athletics Coaches Association***

"*Author* W. Scott Jones does a fantastic job of recounting how college football and high school football recruiting is a religion in the South. He adequately describes the recruiting process and the under-the-table bribes that took place back in the earlier days of college football prior to NIL, while showing the impact and influence that a high school coach has on their players. A novel that is a must-read for all football fans past and present."— ***Jeff***

Barnes, Former player at the University of South Carolina (1999-2003), Athletic Director at Hammond School, Columbia, South Carolina.

“It's time to add W. Scott Jones to the list of great Southern authors! Jones knows which words to use and more importantly-when; leaving readers anxious for the next page…chapter…novel.”— ***Brian Jackson, Former player at Clemson University (1988)- Award winning High School Coach and Educator***

“Author W. Scott Jones’ novel, What a Crowd is an excellent read. He has a gift of storytelling that makes you want to know more. This novel brought back so many wonderful memories.”- ***Keith West, Former QB at Wake Forest University 1992- Hall of Fame Educator and Coach.***

“There is no better storyteller than W. Scott Jones. He truly has a gift that few can match. This is a story worth reading.”—***Jay Frye, Former player at the University of South Carolina (1980-1984), Hall of Fame Head Football Coach and Educator***

“What a Crowd is a terrific novel, one that will entertain football fans and will be familiar to those who know how major college football recruiting operates. It's a wonderful life lesson of overcoming racial stereotypes, showing humbleness, humility, and staying true to yourself when the world least expects it.”— ***Joe Cashion, Play-by Play announcer for Coastal Carolina University.***

“Author W. Scott Jones does a wonderful job of weaving fiction with historical facts and figures to magnify the essence of a time when high school football in the South was still pure. An absolute gem for high school and college football fans. Great read!—***Steve Flynn, Defensive Coordinator, Newberry College***

Excerpt:

This was my first encounter with college football's best salesmen. As each of them did their song and dance, I was amazed by their different sales tactics along with their different personalities.

WHAT A CROWD

W. Scott Jones

Moonshine Cove Publishing, LLC
Abbeville, South Carolina U.S.A.

Moonshine Cove Edition Feb 2024

ISBN: 9781952439759

Library of Congress LCCN: 2024902877

Cover image used with the author's permission, back cover design and interior design by Moonshine Cove staff.

About the Author

W. Scott Jones is a semi-retired high school educator and football coach. He has served in various public and private schools in South Carolina during his long career in education. A former Social Studies Teacher of the Year, Coach Jones has also been blessed to serve as a Head Football Coach and Athletic Director; receiving numerous awards. Selected to coach in the Shrine Bowl of the Carolinas in 2010, Coach Jones has been fortunate to be a part of many championship teams along with many outstanding players and wonderful coaches. He has self- published two novels- *A Storm in the Carolinas* (2021) and *The Treasures of a Carolina Summer* (2022). Both novels have received favorable reviews.

Born in Alapaha, Georgia, Coach Jones grew up in a rural area near Sumter, South Carolina. He is a graduate of the University of South Carolina. When he is not writing novels, you will find him traveling, playing golf, attending sporting events, and looking for hidden historical treasures. He loves meeting and interacting with people - especially the veterans of our great nation. His passions have always centered around thc underdogs of life, awkward family dynamics, US history, and uplifting stories; all reflected in his writings.

Coach Jones has been married for thirty plus years to Bridget, who is a successful Licensed Professional Counselor. They have been blessed with three grown children and a labradoodle named Jumping Jasper. Follow Coach Jones at:

Website: (www.wscottjonesauthor.com)

Facebook: (W. Scott Jones Author),

Instagram:(@w.scott_jones_author) X: (@coachsjones)

Foreword

Set in the Deep South, where football has always been a religion, Coach W. Scott Jones' captivating narrative, *What a Crowd*, takes you back to a time long before online recruiting services and NIL deals.

This is the story of the recruiting process of Frankie Lake, the nation's No. 1 football prospect in 1985, and the coach, Stephen Blake, who gets caught up in the process—so to speak—in his staunch support of Lake. Amidst racial tension and recruiting misdeeds, including the kidnapping of a college coach, the country's top high school prospect must decide—and soon—where he'll play college football.

As legendary college football names often come calling—which college will Frankie Lake sign with?

Patrick Garbin, University of Georgia Football Historian, Writer and Author

Preface

Although the stories associated with this novel are fictitious, they are a culmination of years of interactions that I have had with various players and coaches. During my coaching career, I was very fortunate to meet and interact with most of the college coaches mentioned in this novel. When I was a young man, I did not fully appreciate them and what they meant to the great game of football. I am now at a point in my life where I am truly honored to have been a part of a profession which I believe is more than a job- it is a calling. It is my hope that no matter your age- you will appreciate this fictitious account which unfolds many truths.

This novel would have never been written without the help of the wonderful women in my life. Mrs. Liz Simon, my editor, continues to be a blessing for me. She not only edits my work- she pushes me to continue my writing journey with her amazing positive attitude. Thank you, Liz. Macaylee Jones- thank you again for another amazing book cover and for guiding your father with your expertise. Skylar Jones- thank you for always offering your father sound advice and for listening to me complain. Bridget Jones- thank you for being my rock and soulmate all these years. I love you and thank you for supporting me on this journey. Most importantly- I thank all of the readers that have taken the time to read my work. This is my greatest honor. I always look forward to hearing from you and visiting with you at events.

Prologue

"On the East Coast, football is a cultural experience. In the Midwest, it's a form of cannibalism. On the West Coast, it's a tourist attraction. And in the South, football is a religion, and Saturday is the holy day."

Coach Marino Casem, Southern University

I remember reaching down to pick up a yellow blocking dummy from the sidelines of the practice field. Before I dragged the heavy waterlogged bag to my drill area, I looked around to see if any of the other assistant coaches on my staff had brought out the rest of the equipment. Usually, Spring football practice at Coosawhatchie County High School in the Lowcountry of South Carolina was supposed to be a time to review fundamentals and a time to look at the upcoming talent. On this particular day, May 13, 1985, I knew that something was different. My boss, Head Football Coach Bill Hanover, had told us early that morning in a staff meeting that he wanted more pep in our step at practice. He also warned us that we could either be enthusiastic at practice or some of us would be enthusiastically fired. He further stated, "Y'all better be gettin' after it or you can take the next Greyhound bus that leaves this town."

Everyone knew that Coach Hanover was a tough man on his players and his coaches. I had already witnessed him fire two assistants the year before. One of the assistants briefly dozed off during a Saturday morning meeting while we were breaking down the next opponent's game film. When Coach Hanover saw him snoring, the assistant was fired on the spot. Another assistant was fired during the season when he walked out to the practice field wearing sunglasses and flip flops. He too, was immediately let go.

I had made up my mind that I was going to be more enthusiastic and focused than I had ever been. I had no intention of being fired. I was a second-year high school football coach and teacher at the rural South Carolina school. I was determined to make a name for myself and climb the steep ladder of the coaching profession. As the only African American coach on the staff there were many times when I felt that I had to prove my worth more so than the other white coaches. I didn't mind the hard work, in fact, I had chosen to come to what my grandmother described as a God forsaken marshland in the middle of nowhere.

Coosawhatchie County pronounced (Coos-a-hatchie) was situated a good stone's throw away from Beaufort, thirty minutes from Hilton Head, forty minutes from Savannah, and an hour away from Charleston. The small town of Coosawhatchie was established by trappers in the 1700's. This small town and the surrounding county were named for an extinct tribe of Native Americans called the Coosa who once roamed the same land. The early settlement was burned to the ground by British forces during the Revolutionary War. During the American Civil War, General Robert E. Lee set up his headquarters here when he was in charge of the South Carolina defenses of the Lowcountry. At the end of the Civil War, much of the town was burned down again as Union General William T. Sherman came through the area.

With its marshy lands much of the county never developed like its coastal neighbors. However, because its proximity was so close to the coast some residents derived their income from the coastal fishing industries, mainly the harvesting of oysters and shrimp. Those who made a living from the ocean were classified as either boat owners, deck mates, pluckers, shuckers, or shellers. Most everyone else who lived there worked in agriculture; mainly family farms that had been handed down for generations. Some people also worked in the timber industry while a few worked in small shops or various other business ventures.

A vast majority of the residents were poor or middle class. There were a handful of prominent families descended from generational wealth which owned most of the businesses and significant properties. The educational gap between the haves and have nots was as different as their bank accounts.

Situated not far from the Georgia state line and crisscrossed by Interstate 95, the county was popular for out of state tourists on their way to and back from Florida. After World War II, it became increasingly popular to those tourists who could not legally purchase fireworks from their home state. Businesses that sold fireworks in Coosawhatchie County generated a considerable amount of income. Long before there was an interstate, Coosawhatchie County tried to promote itself as the Cheapest Fireworks Capital of the World. Many people from Savannah and some as far away as Richmond, Virginia bought their fourth of July sparklers and firecrackers from vendors in the county who sold their merchandise at a ridiculous reduced price.

The darkest side of the economy was illegal drug smuggling from the coast to Interstate 95. Drug abuse itself was no different than any other place, but the drug traffic that came with it was a constant concern for law enforcement. In a not so far-fetched tale, some of the local people used to say that crime was always hard to solve in Coosawhatchie County because everyone had the same DNA and there were only a few viable dental records available; with no practicing dentist or dental clinic in town.

I knew all about the place when I took the job at Coosawhatchie. However, my choice to work for such a tough football coach was a no-brainer for me because Coach Bill Hanover was one of the most successful coaches in the Lowcountry of South Carolina. I was very surprised when he said to me during my interview, “Stephen, I think you will feel right at home here at our school. Your college coach at the Citadel told me that Stephen Blake was one of the hardest workers he had ever coached. Coach Blake, I would be honored to have you join our staff."

Many of my preconceived notions about the man were dismissed after I was hired. I had assumed that since Coach Hanover grew up as a white man in a small Southern town, he talked with a dialect which made him at times seem backwards, and because he dressed like a country bumpkin, he was one of those old racist- Redneck guys. After working for him and getting to know him, my first impressions of him were far off the mark.

It was often said in the coaching community that Coach Hanover, during his career, literally willed his teams to win some of the games they should have lost. His football teams were known for a tough defensive style of play where the object was to get in the backfield of the opposition and create what he called a "Tornado of Ass Whoopin'. His offensive strategy was simple: Do not fumble the ball and slam the "tater" right down the throats of the opposition. To him, he thought a reverse or trick play was cheating. Over the years, whenever one of his assistant coaches tried to show him a new offensive strategy or try to convince him to put in a gimmick play, he would always listen and then without fail, he would always growl, "The game of football was meant to be a battle, not some Broadway play." And whenever he did pass the ball, it was so rare, his receivers were always wide open.

Coach Hanover was a unique individual of complex simplicity. I soon learned that he had returned to his hometown after serving as a Marine in the Korean War. The Purple Heart recipient was sent home a hero after being shot three times by a Chinese soldier sporting a SKS semi-automatic rifle. The Chinese soldier who shot him and two of his North Korean buddies was killed by Coach Hanover when he clubbed them to death with the butt of his rifle. Almost dying on the battlefield, Coach Hanover felt like he was the luckiest man in the world when he returned home and was asked to coach at his alma mater after an unexpected coaching vacancy. He became the Head Football Coach of Coosawhatchie County High School in 1954.

Once considered one of the best linebackers to ever come out of the small town, "Bowlegged Bill" Hanover received his nickname as a child because he was so bowlegged it appeared that it was a miracle that he could walk much less run. His nickname became immortalized in the community when he came back from Korea and was asked by a local reporter about his experience in the war. Coach Hanover simply said, "Aw, hell, they shot me with a BB gun, that's why I survived."

Although his friends always called him "B.B." there wasn't a player or coach at Coosawhatchie that dared call him that to his face. As a former Drill Sergeant in the Marines, Coach Hanover had a vocabulary that at times was so vile, there weren't many in the town who had the ability to translate his vicious use of the English language spattered with various words of Korean slang. He jumbled his words together with a Lowcountry accent which was so thick, some people from out of town confused him as a displaced Bostonian sailor. There were quite a few in the community who didn't want to know what he occasionally hollered. Some of them were scared to death of the man who had acquired a reputation of saying what he thought and being able to physically back up what he said.

By the time I began to know him, he was still a physical specimen of a man who would occasionally show his players that he could still lift just as much as them on any given day. He looked like Coach Erk Russell, the famous longtime University of Georgia Defensive Coordinator, who had recently become the Head Football Coach at Georgia Southern. The only difference in the way they looked, was that Coach Hanover had a patch of grey hair on the back of his head.

Former players from Coach Hanover's early years of coaching privately shared stories about the times where he would dress out with only a helmet and pulverize any young man that dared to challenge him on the football field. Many of them had witnessed on more than one occasion, Coach Hanover whipping a few men in the community, who dared to challenge his authority as the Athletic Director of the school. The most famous scuffle happened in 1959 after a home basketball game. Five of the biggest rednecks in town stood in the parking lot of the school and tried to attack a referee, who they thought had made several bad calls. Coach Hanover knew them all, and warned them to leave before he had them arrested. When one of the men threw a sucker punch at Coach Hanover that fool and his buddies made a horrible mistake. By the time the deputies of the Coosawhatchie Sheriff's Department arrived on the scene, Coach Hanover stood over the ravaged bodies of the five idiots, who were missing a few teeth and bleeding like they had been attacked by a wild crocodile.

Because of his strange accent and his gruff demeanor many people assumed Coach Hanover was uneducated. They were mistaken. Bill Hanover always loved to read a good novel, enjoyed the information he read in every edition of Newsweek magazine, and was considered by many in the community an expert on military history. Through the years, many of the locals had asked him to run for political office; however, each time when asked, he would always say, "No thanks. I'm just a football coach. That's all I'll ever be."

His most famous line was, "I un told ya once...I tell ya once more and the hammer done come." Whenever he said those words, everyone knew he meant it. After saying those words once to a defensive end named James Hayes, during a rainy-day practice in the gym, Coach Hanover applied a flipper with his forearm across the young man's chest and sent him two rows into the bleachers. After picking up the young man and making sure he wasn't injured, the entire team stood in awe of their coach and his powerful forearms. That lick he applied to James Hayes became almost as legendary as his heroic survival in Korea.

Coach Hanover believed that weight training was overrated. However, when his teams did lift weights he only allowed his players to squat and do variations of the overhead press. He preferred to strengthen his players by making them bear crawl 50 yards and then turn around and duck walk back another 50 yards. He loved one-on-one competitions of tug of war and once joked that his teams could last into the fourth quarter because of a drill he called the "Sidewinder."

The practice field which was nothing more than an old pasture, sat next to a cotton field. Coach Hanover would take his team to the cotton field and they would have to sprint in between the plowed-up rows. Whenever he blew his whistle, they would begin running as fast as they could. Then after a few yards, he would yell, "Hoppin' John Time." This meant the players had to hop back and forth over the cotton plants which in the summer were about three feet tall. In a few seconds the entire team would be out of breath. By the time that field's cotton harvest was picked, the ten rows next to the practice field were damaged and practically barren. It was once said that the farmer, who lost the annual ten rows of cotton, could have charged Coach Hanover a small fortune for his losses, but he, like the coach, wanted the players to be in tip top shape. The farmer never had a problem with the "Sidewinder."

Whenever a player forgot to put up his equipment and left it on the floor of the locker room after a practice or a game, that player would then meet the wrath of Coach Hanover. He would administer licks with a thick paddle he called, "Old Reminder." Another of his famous lines was, "No punishment here, only reminders."

There were times when Coach Hanover wanted to make a point at practice. To accomplish this, he would carry out "Old Reminder" with him and administer licks to linemen who missed a blocking assignment. He never paddled his skill players; only the linemen. During the first year of school integration in 1971, a black school administrator once warned him that he better not use the paddle on any of the black players. Coach Hanover laughed and said, "The day I stop whoopin' ass is the day you can have my job."

Although he was feared by his players and his coaches, his positive influence on them was immeasurable. He definitely had a big bark, but Coach Hanover was known to help many in the community when nobody was looking. He once personally paid for the funeral of the mother of a player whose family didn't have insurance. There were a few late nights where he would drive his pickup out into the utmost rural areas of Coosawhatchie County. He loved to surprise poor families with a mess of fish or a box of fresh garden vegetables. Every person who benefited from his generosity would later tell others that Coach Hanover told them that he found the items on the side of the road.

Coach Hanover grew up poor on the farm, and whenever he saw a child that needed food, clothing, or shoes, it wasn't uncommon for him to pass his hat around the local barber shop or the local churches for donations. During the winter months, he spent almost every afternoon visiting the homes of his players. Sometimes driving as far as twenty miles he made it a priority to actually go into the homes and visit with parents or grandparents. Once inside the homes, he always ate what was offered including opossum and racoon. He was never too good to take a few sips of whiskey or moonshine. He also used the home visits to observe living conditions to determine which family needed more assistance with the basics of humanity like food, clothing, clean water, heating or cooling. By 1975, Coach Hanover was the most trusted white man in the black community.

* * *

On this rather warm day in May, I couldn't wait for practice to begin. I had arranged for a fellow teacher to watch my 7th period World History class so that I would be the first coach to make it to the practice field. It was the first day of live contact drills. Although I knew all of the players on the team, I, like the other coaches, was anxious to see which of the younger players would stand out. After coming off a moderately successful season of nine wins, expectations in Coosawhatchie were on the rise because the junior varsity team had gone undefeated the year before and because of a rising senior player nicknamed "Running Waters." The player's real name was Frankie Lake. Frankie had started the year before as a defensive end that nobody could seem to block. He was a late bloomer on the football field, not because of his athletic ability, but because he had a hard time remembering his right from his left.

When two of the starting halfbacks were injured in the eighth game of the prior season, Coach Hanover inserted Frankie into the backfield. The 6'3, 205-pound raw athlete, literally began running around and over the competition. The first time he touched the ball in a game Frankie ran right up the middle almost untouched. He was untouched because he spun off a defender, who had made his way into our backfield. Frankie ran almost twenty yards in five different directions before he broke the line of scrimmage. While Coach Hanover was screaming for him to slam it in the middle of the line; Frankie put on a show of athleticism that nobody that night had ever seen. Later when looking over the game film, our coaches noticed that Franke had avoided the attempted tackles of all eleven defenders. After he scored, the jubilant Franke ran off the field to Coach Hanover and said,

"Coach, don't cuss me, but when I see daylight I promise I'll always score."

On that night, Frankie carried the ball only eleven more times. He set a school rushing record with 401 yards and six touchdowns, while playing every snap at defensive end. At the end of the third quarter, Frankie collapsed near the sideline. The team's physician thought he could possibly be having a heat stroke. Dr. Claude Davis, a local veterinarian, checked Frankie's temperature with a rectal thermometer on the sidelines. Several players surrounded the physician and Frankie so that the crowd could not see Frankie's bare bottom. When Dr. Davis determined that Frankie was "just a little tired," Coach Hanover pulled Frankie up and said, "Your engine just needs to cool down a bit. You're good."

That night, Coach Hanover and everyone in Coosawhatchie realized that Frankie Lake was a special player; one you rarely have a chance to witness in real life. Gerald Davis, of the *Lowcountry Times,* wrote the headline: Lake Makes a Big Splash. In his sports article he wrote, "The junior running back looked like "running waters" as he glided effortlessly through the opposing defense which looked like a dam with a big crack."

Frankie was a natural athlete. He was also dirt poor and stronger than any man in Coosawhatchie County. He had been raised to assist his father who cut and hauled pulpwood for a living. Frankie didn't need a weight room, he had been lifting heavy limbs and rolling pine stumps since he was eight-years old. He had a light complexion, and a reddish tone to his skin and hair. Some of his family gave the African American teenager the nickname, "Red." After several local news articles about his athletic achievements, he became known by everyone in the area. Because of his new-found fame, his new nickname for everyone in Coosawhatchie County became - Running Waters. In only a few weeks, Frankie Lake went from being a country boy that very few people knew anything about to a sports hero for a town that loved football as if it were a part of its official religion.

If Frankie had not sprained his ankle during our second-round playoff game that season, everyone in Coosawhatchie knew that we would have won the state championship. An entire community waited patiently for the return of a new-found hero during the winter months knowing that a run at the state championship was a reality if Frankie Lake was healthy and ready to suit up on 'Friday nights.'

Because our school was located in the middle of nowhere and because Frankie had excelled in a limited number of games his junior year, he wasn't listed as a national recruit. That's until, Gerald Davis of the *Lowcountry Times,* reached out and contacted Tom Lemming, who had become known for his national publication called the Tom Lemming Prep Football Report. Mr. Lemming took the advice of his old friend, Gerald Davis and listed Frankie Lake as an honorable mention. This led to Frankie being listed in the prestigious Max Emfinger Recruiting Service, which every college coach began using as the gospel of where to find hidden talent. Frankie didn't make it into Joe Terranova's *Top 80 High School Football Recruits* or Allen Wallace's new *Super Prep Magazine*, but word of his athletic talent was soon making its way through the college football recruiting landscape.

Chapter One

After pulling two more large blocking dummies across the practice field, I could barely hear someone whistling. When I turned around, I was startled when I saw the head football coach of Clemson University, Danny Ford, laying on top of another blocking dummy. He was about fifteen yards away from me, but I could see him clearly. After he finished whistling, Coach Ford put a long stalk of Bahia grass in his mouth and acted like he was smoking a cigar. Before I could say a word, Coach Ford greeted me by saying, "You tell Coach B.B. that he needs to get one of y'all to cut the grass on this practice field. I have cows back in Clemp-son that would love this pasture."

I didn't know if I should respond as I walked closer to the young coach who was already famous for winning the College Football National Championship four years before. I was shocked to find Coach Ford on the practice field.

Coach Ford continued, "Dang, Coach Blake, I'm just foolin' with ya." The very popular coach from the Upstate South Carolina university leaned forward, extended his hand and stated, "If you don't remember, I'm Coach Ford, but my friends call me Danny."

I noticed that the famous coach was wearing blue jeans, a faded orange cotton shirt, and an orange Clemson hat with only a white colored block C on it. Surprised that Coach Ford remembered my name, I replied, "I better not tell Coach Hanover that you said the grass needs some attention. We both know he would make me cut this field after practice tonight."

Coach Ford nodded and replied, "I understand. Coach B.B. is a hard man. What he does here at this small school is amazin'. Everyone says that Coach McKissick at Summerville is the Master of high school football coaching in this state, but I'm here to tell you that Coach Hanover ranks right up there with the football Godfather himself."

I laughed before saying, "Coach, I have to be honest with you. I can't believe you remember me. I've only met you one time before today."

"Shoot, Coach Blake, how could I forget you? Everyone around this state knows you had a pretty good career at the Citadel before you busted your knee."

"Thank you, sir. I sure didn't think anyone remembered me playing."

"Ah, hell, you may not remember this, but I saw you play the night y'all lost to North Savannah when you were in high school. I ain't gonna lie to you, I wasn't there to watch you, but after the game you played that night, we were definitely interested until, well, you know... We had a fullback from Georgia who was just a tad bit taller, a tad bit heavier, and a whole lot faster than you. While you were still on our radar, that young man from Georgia surprised us and decided that he wanted to come to Clemp-son." Before I could respond, Coach Ford raised up from the blocking dummy and said, "Look who has decided to join the party today."

I looked across the field and saw two men walking toward us. One was dressed in all black and the other one was dressed in all orange. Coach Ford laughed before saying, "The University of South Carolina was very smart when they hired Joe Morrison." He paused for a few seconds before saying, "And just between you and me, Coach Morrison is going to make my life difficult." He paused again, took a deep breath and said, "Coach Blake, I hope you can keep this a secret, because I would call you the biggest liar in town if someone said that I really didn't like Coach Majors at Tennessee."

"Your secret is safe with me, Coach Ford, but I thought all you big-time college coaches were friends."

"Johnny is a good man and I love him to death, but he has been a pain in my side when it comes to recruiting. He and his staff work their tails off. Johnny Majors is the ultimate professional and everyone in college football knows that he is hard to beat." He then paused momentarily before saying, "You know the NCAA is talkin' 'bout not allowin' the college head football coaches to visit schools anymore like we do now. I have a feeling it won't be long until they end this for everyone."

With the ringing of the school day's last bell, I could barely hear Coach Joe Morrison from the University of South Carolina when he walked up to Coach Ford, reached down and shook his hand. The former NFL player, who had a stellar career with the New York Giants peered over his Ray-Ban Aviator sunglasses saying, "I told Johnny when I saw him in the parking lot that I wouldn't be surprised if you were already here promising that Lake kid a new car or new house."

Coach Ford laughed and glanced at me before replying, "You must have me mistaken for Coach Majors. We don't have a bank filled with gold like they have at Fort Knox-ville at the University of Tennessee."

I immediately looked at Coach Majors waiting for his reaction. Without hesitation, Coach Majors replied, "You know we do everything by the book just like you, Danny."

Coach Ford laughed before saying, "Touché... I just love to get under your skin, Coach."

Coach Majors declared, "I don't know if any of you have seen this Lake kid in person, but I'm here to tell you that he looks like a Greek god. We don't have anyone on our roster at Tennessee who looks like him. If any of us was ever going to break the rules, that young man would tempt all of us."

Coach Ford then pointed across the field while saying, "Well, it looks like we have a lot of company here today in the middle of nowhere."

We all turned and could plainly see Coach Bobby Bowden from Florida State, Coach Joe Paterno from Penn State, and Coach Bo Schembechler from Michigan walking toward us. Walking behind them were another group of coaches including Coach Earl Bruce from Ohio State, Coach Vince Dooley from Georgia, his brother, Bill Dooley from Virginia Tech, along with Coach Pat Dye from Auburn. Behind all of them were all the assistant coaches who had accompanied their head coach. Coach Ford whispered to me, "All of them assistant coaches are the chauffeurs."

By the time the hoard of college coaches had made their way across the field, I could see Coach Hanover, the rest of the Coosawhatchie assistant coaches, and the entire team jogging out of the locker room toward the practice field. Before I had a chance to shake the hands of all of the college head coaches, I ran over to the far end zone to listen to what Coach Hanover was telling our players before practice began. Once I approached the team, I could see that all of them were on one knee listening to Coach Hanover. I noticed that Coach Hanover looked more unprofessional than usual. He had not shaved and what he was wearing made him look like he was about to change the oil in his truck. One of the best high school coaches' in the state was dressed in a pair of paint stained khaki shorts and a plain white cut off t-shirt filled with holes. Making him look even worse - his belly slightly hung over his shorts. He looked like the biggest redneck in town.

I then heard Coach Hanover say, "Now all you know we have some guests up in here to watch our practice. Be on your best behavior, show 'em what you can do, and if I see one of you eyeballin' one of those college coaches I'll give you a taste of 'Old Reminder' in front of everyone here. Now let's get after it today."

When he finished, Coach Hanover then motioned for me to come closer. When I walked over to him, Coach Hanover said,

"Coach Blake, I want you to go over there and tell Coach Ford to get his ass off my practice field. You tell him I said that nobody lays on my damn practice field."

For the first time in my career, I hesitated and questioned the order I had been given by my head coach. I quickly asked, "Coach, are you sure you want me to tell Coach Ford to get off the field? I don't know..."

Coach Hanover interrupted me and yelled, "You're damn right I do. I want you to tell him to get his ass off my practice field! I want you to tell him just like that. If I find out that you didn't tell him in my exact words, you can kiss your career here goodbye. Now go on over there and tell him what I said."

I didn't want to tell Danny Ford to get up off the practice field. I couldn't believe that Coach Hanover had put me in such an awkward position. I also didn't want to embarrass Coach Ford in front of the other coaches.

By the time I was twenty yards away from Coach Ford, I could see that Coach Joe Paterno from Penn State had knelt down beside Coach Ford. It appeared that they were having a private conversation. I slowed down my pace toward them, not wanting to interrupt, but when I heard Coach Hanover yell, "Hurry up, Coach Blake," I knew I had to speed up and deliver the dreaded message. Once I painfully approached Coach Ford, he shouted, "Coach Paterno, have you met the brains behind this operation down here at Coosawhatchie? This is Coach Blake."

Coach Paterno stood up and said, "Eh, I haven't had the pleasure, but Coach Kenney on my staff tells me you're one heck of a young coach."

I didn't know how to respond. I knew Coach Hanover was watching. I wanted to puke. I didn't want to embarrass Coach Ford, and more than anything, I really wanted to have a conversation with the legendary Joe Paterno from Penn State. When I glanced at all of the famous coaches, I knew they would all hear what I had to say. This group of coaches included Coach Bobby Bowden of Florida State, who by now was standing right behind Coach Ford. To avoid conflict, I reluctantly asked Coach Ford, "Coach, can I please have a word with you in private?"

Coach Ford replied, "Why sure, Coach Blake. Kneel on down here and shoot away."

I nervously replied, "No, sir. I need you to walk over here with me."

Coach Bowden whispered loudly to Coach Vince Dooley, "Well, it looks like old Danny already has an inside track to this Lake kid."

Coach Paterno spoke up and said, "I don't know about that."

Coach Ford stood up and smiled before looking at all of the other college head coaches. He then said loudly, "Coach Blake, I sure hope you're here to tell me that Frankie Lake's mother still wants me to stop by the house on my way back to Clemp-son tonight."

As all of the coaches began laughing, I whispered, "No sir, this is a lot more confidential."

Evidently thinking all of the other college head coaches had heard my reply, Coach Ford shouted out, "Go ahead and tell me. We're all friends here. What is so important?"

While I began to speak to the most famous audience in my life, I finally blurted out loudly, "Coach Hanover sent me over here to tell you to get your ass off his practice field. He said nobody lays on his damn practice field."

For about three seconds, I felt like time stood still. For the rest of my life I would never forget the reaction on the faces of some of college football's most famous coaches. I would also never forget the feeling I felt when I realized that the nation's top college coaches, all white men, listened as a young African American assistant football coach at Coosawhatchie County High School reprimanded one of the most famous coaches in the profession. I wished that I could take it all back. Then it happened. Coach Ford began laughing while the other coaches remained silent. Coach Danny Ford yelled out across the practice field, “You've got balls, B. B. You have the biggest balls in this state.” Coach Ford then turned to me and said, “You tell your boss that I would have done the same exact thing. Nobody lays on my practice field up at Clemp-son.”

Once those words came out his mouth, the other college coaches chimed in with laughter and a few words of their own.

Coach Paterno cried out, “Coach Blake, you tell Coach Hanover- much respect from Penn State.”

Coach Vince Dooley shouted, “You tell him he’s my kind of coach.”

Bo Schembechler sneered before yelling, “You tell him he has a job waiting on him at Michigan if he wants one.”

Coach Earl Bruce, yelled louder, “You tell him that both of you have jobs at Ohio State if you want them.”

Coach Bobby Bowden hollered, "Dad gum...Tell him I said that y’all can come to Florida where the weather is a lot better than Ohio State.”

Coach Majors screamed, “Come coach in God’s country in Tennessee.”

Coach Pat Dye yelled at me, “Tell him that I would like to have a word with him right now.”

I was surprised by the reaction of the famous coaches. While the team was still warming up with old fashioned calisthenics, I jogged over to Coach Hanover. Coach Hanover asked me, “Did you tell Coach Ford the way I told you?”

“Yes, sir, I sure did. You didn’t hear him yell at you? He said that you had the biggest balls in this state. All those coaches want to hire you. As a matter of fact, Coach Dye from Auburn wants to speak to you right now.”

Without any noticeable facial reaction Coach Hanover quickly responded, “You go tell Coach Dye that I’m a little busy right now. He can talk to me after practice like the rest of ‘em. Hurry up because we are about to start practice.”

Chapter Two

I could tell that Coach Dye from Auburn University wasn't very pleased with having to wait to meet with Coach Hanover after practice. No matter, I didn't have time to worry about Coach Dye's hurt feelings. I had to hustle to get ready for the first individual period of the practice.

Once our team broke up into individual drills, almost all of the college head coaches walked over to my practice area of the field to witness Frankie Lake. I could see them in my peripheral vision each time I would yell instructions to my players or demonstrate how I wanted them to emulate a certain physical maneuver. In the back of my mind, I was auditioning in front of some of college football's greatest coaches.

For the entire twenty-minute period I had my group of four running backs do basic ball exchange drills and a few agility drills. There wasn't a thing fancy or complicated with what we were doing, yet; once the period was over, I heard Coach Morrison from South Carolina say, "Impressive drills, Coach Blake. I like the way your players move."

I was mesmerized by those words of encouragement from the famous coach. As we jogged over to a team drill which Coach Hanover called, "Hit the Bale of Hay," Coach Majors caught up with me and said, "I'd like to talk to you after practice about the way you teach your running backs to secure the football."

I felt like all of the coaches were just as impressed with my coaching ability as they were with the way Frankie Lake carried the football. My self-confidence as a young coach was at a peak.

When we started the "Hit the Bale of Hay" drill, Frankie came up to me and said, "Coach, this chin strap ain't right."

I gave it a quick look and said, "Go over to the tool kit on the sideline. In the tool box you should be able to find a new snap and a Phillips head screwdriver."

As Frankie ran over to the sidelines, all of the college coaches watched with great anticipation thinking he might be leaving practice. I heard Coach Paterno whisper, "For crying out loud, when are we going to see this kid in action? I sure hope he is going to finish practice."

Coach Dooley from Georgia interceded, "Be patient, Joe. He's fixin' his helmet."

While the college head football coaches were all turned watching Frankie's every move, they all heard what sounded like a loud clap of thunder when rising Senior linebacker Doug Pye knocked the hell out of his "bale of hay" named Willie Sanders. By the time the college head football coaches turned to view what had occurred all they could see was Doug laying on top of Willie who momentarily had the breath knocked out of him.

Coach Bruce from Ohio State reached over and grabbed my arm before asking, "Any chance we can see that young man tackle again? I can't remember when I've heard such a collision."

I replied, "No problem, Coach. Everyone on the team has to hit the bale of hay three times before Coach Hanover finishes this drill."

The "bale of hay" as Coach Hanover called it was a player who had to stand behind an orange highway warning cone. He was instructed not to move while another player stood five yards away waiting to run at full speed and tackle the "bale of hay." Coach Hanover would yell out, "Sick 'em." The only thing the "bale of hay" could do was to tighten up and protect himself as best as possible.

To all of the college head coaches this drill seemed as backward as anything they had ever witnessed. But Coach Hanover was convinced that this drill alone made his players tougher than most. He also believed it weeded out the ones who would eventually give in when the going became tough. The drill was brutal.

With great interest, all of the college head coaches watched as Doug Pye walked back up for his final turn to hit the bale of hay. This time, before the next bale of hay stepped up for duty, Coach Hanover yelled, "Hold up. Where the hell is Frankie?"

Before anyone could speak, Frankie ran through the hoard of college coaches and cried out, "Right here, Coach. Ready to go."

Frankie snapped his new chinstrap buckle in place and took his turn as the bale of hay to the amazement of every college coach who had traveled to watch the star of Coosawhatchie run the ball. None of the college coaches could believe that Coach Hanover was going to allow his best player to be hammered by a linebacker in a most vulnerable position.

I heard Coach Majors whisper to Coach Schembechler, "There is no way I would allow my thoroughbred to take a lick like he's about to take. Coach Hanover is riskin' the whole franchise."

Several seconds later, the loudest sound ever recorded in Coosawhatchie since the Civil War was heard by everyone in attendance. It sounded like Robert E. Lee's old cannon in front of the courthouse steps was being fired. People to this day describe the sound in different ways. One former player said that the collision sounded like a speeding freight train hitting a gasoline truck. Boom!

To the surprise of everyone, including Coach Hanover, Frankie Lake didn't budge. It had to be one of the most incredible hits witnessed in the game of football. Doug Pye, the toughest redneck in Coosawhatchie, lay at the feet of Frankie Lake with the facemask of his helmet squarely planted in the sod. For a second or two, most everyone in attendance thought that poor Doug was dead. It was as if Doug had run full speed into a telephone pole and the telephone pole didn't budge an inch. With great jubilation and excitement, everyone started clapping when Doug popped up from the ground and shook Frankie's hand. Doug cried out, "Running Waters is one tough dude."

The lick Doug Pye put on Frankie Lake was a failure in the eyes of Coach Hanover, because a tackle wasn't made. However, that lick turned out to be successful and made a lasting impression on the college coaches for both Doug and Frankie.

When the drill concluded, Coach Hanover hollered, "Oh Boy Time" which meant it was time for a water break. As the players ran fifty yards to the edge of the practice field, they drank one-by-one out of an old hose pipe. During the water break, Coach Ford walked up to me and said, "Those two studs need to come to Clemp-son. I have a feeling that those boys will listen to what you have to say, since you're one of the best coaches out here."

I was flattered by what I was hearing. Coach Ford then stated, "I hope that you and I can grab something to eat before I leave tonight."

"Sure thing, Coach. We have one place that has some of the best pulled pork ever."

Coach Hanover then shouted for me. In a sprint, I caught up with my boss. Coach Hanover said, "We are going to work on team offense for about thirty minutes to end this show. Keep Frankie out the first few plays. I'll let you know when to put him in."

"Yes, sir."

On my way back to the middle of the practice field, Coach Bobby Bowden walked over to me and asked, "Hey, Coach, how would you like to come to FSU this summer and work at my football camp? We would love to have you and Frankie come and visit with us. Good food, good fellowship, and good pay. I'll talk with you after practice, and we can nail down the dates."

Before I could respond, Coach Joe Morrison interrupted Coach Bowden and said, "Coach Blake, I sure would like to take you out to eat after practice. I would like to talk to you about your running back drills. I love the way your players respond."

Coach Bowden broke back into the conversation by saying, "I'd love to hear your thoughts as well. Is there a good place where we can eat and talk?"

I smiled and replied, "The best pulled pork barbeque in this state is at Henry's Barbeque about three blocks down the road. You can't miss it. It's right across from a seafood restaurant called the Big Fish and a steakhouse called the Lowcountry Sizzler. If you would rather have seafood, or a good steak, both are pretty good as well."

Coach Bowden made an executive decision saying, "I think barbeque would be the best choice."

Before I could walk away from the college coaches, the offensive line coach from Tennessee came up to me and said, "Coach Blake, I'm sorry to interrupt you, but my name is Coach Phillip Fulmer. I'll be assigned to your school this fall to recruit your players. I just wanted to say hello."

Interrupting Coach Fulmer, another college assistant coach spoke to me and stated, "I'm Coach Ken Treadway from Virginia Tech. I also wanted to meet you as I was just told by Coach Dooley that this will be my home away from home this upcoming season. I know you're busy, but do you know where I can find the nearest liquor store in this town?"

When I didn't immediately reply to him, Coach Treadway quickly said, "The liquor is not for me. Coach Fulmer wanted to know."

Coach Fulmer yelled, "The hell I did!"

Coach Treadway yelled back, "Ok, Phil. Whatever you say. You don't have to hide your drinking from Coach Blake. We all know about you and Coach Majors." Coach Treadway then laughed loud before saying, "I love to watch Phil get mad at me. He and Coach Majors are as straight-laced as they come on the recruiting trail. Everyone knows that I am always the practical joker."

* * *

When Coach Hanover blew his whistle, he screamed, "Team time. Team time."

For the next ten minutes the starting offensive unit ran the ball up the middle for six straight plays in a goal line period which seemed brutal. Coach Hanover spotted the ball on the three-yard line after each attempt. Whenever the offense was stopped short of the goal line, he would blow his whistle and the offense would have to sprint to the other goal line and back. After two full field sprints, Frankie Lake yelled at his teammates, "Don't get mad at Coach, score and we ain't got to run."

After the seventh play of the scrimmage, Coach Paterno walked over to me and asked, "What's the deal? We need to see the Lake kid run the ball, for crying out loud."

I didn't respond, but when I looked at all the other college coaches I could tell that they were becoming impatient as well. After the next play I walked up to Coach Hanover and asked, "Do you want me to put in Frankie, now?"

Coach Hanover shouted, mixing in a sentence of Korean saying, "Naega chaeg-imjaya." Nobody could understand a word Coach Hanover was saying until he screamed, "I dun told you, I'll let you know when to put him in."

He then stomped away from me like a mad man, throwing down his cap and kicking the ground with his black Spot-Bilt coaching shoes. He suddenly turned around and screamed, "44 Iso. Run it again and block the damn four technique this time."

After the offense scored, Coach Hanover then yelled, "Frankie, get in."

As Frankie jogged into the huddle, Coach Hanover shouted, "Riverside! Riverside! Turn it around." He then picked up the ball and placed it on the ten-yard line before screaming, "We have five plays to go ninety yards. If we don't score, there will be hell to pay. Five plays is all you get."

While the offense ran to the line of scrimmage and became set, I looked at all of the college coaches who were all looking at Frankie Lake with great anticipation. Words could never paint a picture of the athletic skill Frankie Lake displayed when he received a simple handoff from the I formation and took off toward the right side of the line. When he jumped over the defensive end, the entire group of college coaches stood in disbelief. When he sidestepped a linebacker and reversed field, the gang of college coaches followed down the field like they were following a celebrity. As soon as Frankie hit full stride at the opposite 40-yard line, every college coach shook their heads, smiled, and knew they had witnessed something very special. While Frankie was being mobbed by his offensive teammates in the end zone, I was being mobbed by the college coaches who had seen all they needed to see.

Coach Schembechler from Michigan ran up to me, grabbed my arm and said, "Do you have a record of his 40 time? That young man may be the fastest kid on the planet."

Before I could answer, Coach Paterno interrupted and asked, "Is anyone filming this scrimmage? I want a copy of the film."

Coach Bruce shouted, "You go ahead and tell that young man that he has a full-ride at Ohio State."

Coach Bowden shoved Coach Bruce aside and yelled, "Dad gum it, you go ahead and tell that youngin' that he is the number one prospect at Florida State."

* * *

We only scrimmaged for about ten more plays. Frankie Lake didn't touch the ball the rest of the day, but it was all right. The college coaches had seen enough to know that Frankie Lake would be their number one priority. Although they still had their sights on the nation's top recruits, like Todd Ellis, a quarterback from

Greensboro, North Carolina or a running back named Brian Davis, from Washington, Pennsylvania, on this particular day, some of college football's most prestigious coaches had witnessed perfection which had them sold.

While they all waited to speak with the newly, most sought-after recruit in the nation, I could hear some of them making plans and scheming on how they could make Coosawhatchie County High School their home away from home. I heard Coach Paterno tell his assistant, Coach Kenney, "You better find yourself a good place to stay in this town because you will be here at least once or twice a week until we get him to sign with us. That kid is unbelievable."

Coach Ford walked over to me and said, "Don't forget about us going out to eat after this is over."

I nervously replied, "I'm afraid we'll have some company eating with us."

I then explained that some of the other college coaches had asked me to discuss my running back drills over dinner.

"No problem. I already know you're one heck of a coach. I just want to know more about you, Coach Blake."

The scene outside of Coach Hanover's office after practice could only be described as chaotic. College coaches, holding notepads, lined the hallway which led to the football locker room and the head football coach's office at Coosawhatchie County High School. Since I was Frankie's position coach, I was asked by Coach Hanover to sit in his office with him and listen as each group of college coaches entered and gave Frankie a three-minute sales pitch on why their school was the best fit for a young man from the middle of nowhere. Franke was polite, smiled the entire time, and never said more than two or three words as each coaching staff came in and did their best to convince the young man to sign with their school. Before the "bidding" began, Coach

Hanover had told all of the coaches they had three minutes to say what was on their mind and then they had to leave.

This was my first encounter with college football's best salesmen. As each of them did their song and dance, I was amazed by their different sales tactics along with their different personalities. Although this wasn't the first time I had ever seen college coaches at Coosawhatchie County High School, it was the largest group I had ever seen on one day. I had only seen many of them on television or had seen their faces in national publications like *Athlon Magazine*. I watched their every move and listened to every word they spoke. I loved it when Johnny Majors of the University of Tennessee knelt down on one knee and said, "Now Franke, you know the only good thing that has ever come out of Alabama is Bear Bryant. Whatever you do, promise me you won't go to Alabama. It's an awful place."

Coach Schembechler from Michigan stood up when he said, "It gets a little cold in Ann Arbor, but when you're playing in the biggest stadium in the nation, by God I'm here to tell you that you never feel the cold."

Coach Bruce from Ohio State in a serious and deep voice said, "Frankie, you have to promise me that you will not go to Michigan. It's the coldest place on the planet. They make some of their football players live in igloos."

Coach Dooley from Georgia said, "Athens is the most beautiful city in the world. There is no other experience like playing between the hedges. You remind me a lot of Herschel Walker when he was your age. I think you may be better than him."

An animated Coach Paterno took a different approach when he said, "I want our players to be a student first and then a football player. We don't have any fancy dorms for the athletes. Your education is the most important thing at Penn State."

Coach Morrison from the University of South Carolina briefly took off his sunglasses and said, "Frankie, this is your home state.

We want young men like you who love South Carolina. Columbia is not that far from here, and your family would have an easy time watching you play."

Coach Dye from Auburn declared, "Now look here. I have no doubt that you will become the next Bo Jackson. I think you may be a little quicker than Bo when he was your age. You need to know that there is nothing that compares to playing a game on the Plains of Auburn."

Coach Dooley, from Virginia Tech said, "I promise you that I'll never lie to you. Our program is built on honesty. We would love for you to be a part of something special at Virginia Tech."

I couldn't help but smile when Coach Bowden from Florida State announced, "Yeah, we think you could be a special player, but most importantly, we want you to graduate and become a good citizen. Don't let all these other coaches fool you. You look like a smart young man. Tallahassee is the place to be."

Out of all the sales pitches, Coach Ford from Clemson was much different when he stated, "Frankie, we obviously think you're a good football player, but at Clemp-son, I want to become your friend. I think you will agree with me that friendship is the most important thing in this world. Twenty years from now, I would like to think that wherever you are in life, you can call me and we'll still be friends."

Once all of the silver-tongued devils had left Coach Hanover's office, Frankie looked at me and said, "I sure hopes they give Doug a scholarship." He then laughed before asking, "Who is Bear Bryant, and is Michigan a long way from here? What is an igloo, 'cause it sounds pretty bad?"

I glanced over at Coach Hanover before I replied, "We'll talk about all this tomorrow. You go ahead and hurry up out of here before your ride leaves you. I bet Doug is ready to go home."

When Frankie walked out of the office, Coach Hanover shut the door before saying, "Now, Coach Blake, you know that there is no way that Frankie will be eligible to play at any of these schools unless he passes the SAT or the ACT this summer. Frankie can tote a football, but he and academics are a different story. I need you to help him with this."

"Yes, sir."

"You need to understand that those college coaches are only interested in one thing. You might think they want you to be their friend, but Coach, I know 'em. They wouldn't piss on you if you were on fiya unless you could help them recruit this boy. I saw how you was talkin' to 'em today. All I'm tellin' you is to be careful."

Chapter Three

Coach Hanover and I could both hear a loud commotion outside of the gym as we approached the exit door. When Coach Hanover opened the door, he realized that the college coaching circus had not ended. Huddled around Frankie and Doug, all of the college coaches were peppering them with questions. The college coaches had been waiting in the parking lot for them to leave campus.

Coach Hanover yelled at the top of his lungs, "Get in your cars and away from my boys!"

After Frankie and Doug drove away, Coach Hanover looked at me and said, "Those college coaches are like vultures."

While driving to Henry's Barbeque, I assumed that most of the college coaches had forgotten about our earlier dinner arrangements as it was almost 7:30 pm. They had not. When I turned into the parking lot of Henry's, I could not believe all the vehicles. When I entered the barbeque joint which was built in 1947 and owned by one of the town's richest men, Henry Bozzard, I couldn't ever remember so many people assembled on a Monday night. Some of the Coosawhatchie faithful had received the news that many of college football's most famous coaches were in town. Those fans piled into the place which also sold more fireworks out of an adjacent building than it did barbeque plates.

The mayor of the town, Eugene Singleton and his third wife, Dora, were there for one reason and one reason only. They wanted the autograph of Coach Joe Morrison. Both graduates of the University of South Carolina, Eugene graduated from there many years before Dora was born. Eugene, who had inherited the only law firm in Coosawhatchie County, seldom did legal work. However, he was known to throw the best dinner parties in town.

As one of the biggest University of South Carolina scholarship donors in the Lowcountry, Eugene and his family had some of the best seats for every University of South Carolina athletic event. He loved the Gamecocks so much, many in town called him Gamecock Gene.

Henry's Barbeque was loud, busy, and it appeared to be out of control. As soon as I entered the door, Coach Ford was the first one to greet me. He said, "We have saved a place for you to sit with us in the back. I hope you don't mind, but I went ahead and ordered you a couple of pulled pork sandwiches and a cold beer."

As I followed Coach Ford to the back of the restaurant, we had to stop several times as local patrons asked Coach Ford for his autograph on their napkins. One lady gave him a hug and cried out, "We love you, Coach Ford, and we love our Tigers."

I quickly noticed that on the other side of the restaurant Coach Morrison from the University of South Carolina was receiving the same adoration from fans who were still celebrating the Gamecocks football team's magical season the year before. It was the same season which gave the University of South Carolina their first ten-win season in the history of the school. The highlight of the season was a close 22-21 victory over their archrival Clemson. Like the rest of the population of South Carolina, the patrons in Henry's Barbeque were equally divided in their loyalty concerning the state's two major universities.

When we finally made our way to the back table in the restaurant, all of the famous college head coaches from around the nation were anxiously waiting for me. For the first time in my life I was the guest of honor. All of the college head coaches made sure to shake my hand and offer me whatever I wanted to eat or drink. Once I was seated, Coach Joe Morrison of South Carolina asked everyone to settle down so he could hear the particulars about how I coached my running backs at Coosawhatchie County High School. For the next ten minutes I tried my best to explain how I coached my players to take a handoff and how I worked with them on ball security. I said nervously, "Coach Hanover hates a fumble."

Coach Bowden exclaimed, "Amen, Brother. There is nothing worse than a dad gum fumble."

Finally, after answering several soft questions about how I coached, Coach Schembechler of Michigan changed the subject when he asked, "Do you have a good relationship with Frankie and the rest of the players?"

"Yes, sir."

Coach Paterno asked, "How long have you known Frankie?"

"Almost two years."

Coach Bruce from Ohio State asked, "Do you think that Frankie trusts you as his coach?"

When I answered, "Yes, sir," I then found myself fielding all kinds of questions. Some of the coaches wanted to know what kind of clothes Frankie liked to wear while others wanted to know what were his favorite foods. A few of them wanted to know what songs and movies he liked and one of them asked what kind of car he liked to drive. It was a free-for-all of many different questions that I could not truthfully answer. It bothered me that not one of the coaches asked anything about Doug Pye.

While I was being interrogated like I was a part of a crime scene, I noticed that the assistant college coaches were rapidly taking many notes; writing in small binders with their school's logo on them. It became apparent to me that the questioning would never end. I finally stood up and said, "Coaches, you will have to excuse me, but I have to go to the restroom."

As I walked toward the restroom I was taken back as some of the college assistant coaches followed me like a bodyguard would do for a celebrity. As I passed by one of the local patrons who was hoping to grab the autograph of one of the college coaches, the older man yelled, "I hear you, Coach Blake. Glad to see these coaches know where to come to learn more about how to play the game of football."

Once inside the one-person restroom, I shut the door, locked it, and wished that I could stay there until all of the college coaches had departed. My mind began racing. I thought about Frankie and his future as a college superstar. I then began to wonder if my ties to Frankie really could land me a job as an assistant college football coach. For a few moments I dreamed of the day I would be a college head coach like Danny Ford or Joe Paterno. Then as I began to zip up my pants, I thought to myself that there would never be a day where a black man in the state of South Carolina would ever be accepted as a college football head coach at one of the big universities.

Facing the reality of the current situation, I reluctantly made my way back to the table. When I sat down next to Danny Ford, I was surprised to see Coach Ford chewing tobacco and spitting the juice on the concrete floor of Henry's. Coach Ford then looked at me and whispered in my ear, "Don't pay attention to any of these jokers. They will sell their soul if they could sign Frankie. Don't get me wrong, I would love for Frankie to sign with us, but I want Frankie to love our program. I don't want him coming to our school if he doesn't love it. I guess that's what makes me different from all of them. They could care less about what Frankie wants."

Then for the next thirty minutes, I listened to all of the college coaches as they talked about various subjects other than the recruitment of Frankie Lake. At one point of the conversation, I could not believe I was listening to Coach Bowden describe his first head coaching job at West Virginia University earlier in his career. When Coach Morrison began talking about his playing days with the New York Giants, everyone stopped and listened. But the highlight of the conversations had to be when Coach Bruce of Ohio State accused Coach Schembechler of Michigan of illegal recruiting. Coach Majors of Tennessee had to separate the two of them before Coach Dooley of Virginia Tech suggested that they both leave as they were creating a scene. Coach Ford laughed loudly and cried out, "That's right, y'all can settle all of this on the field this year."

Coach Bruce turned toward Coach Ford and yelled, "You shut the hell up, Danny. You're the one most responsible for ending Coach Hayes' career at Ohio State in that Gator Bowl game a few years ago."

Coach Ford looked at me and said, "That my friend is a low blow. I didn't tell Coach Woody Hayes to attack and punch my player, Charlie Bauman, on the sidelines at the end of the game. Hell, I didn't even know what happened. I hated that his outburst ended his career."

Coach Vince Dooley of Georgia spoke up and said, "I think it's time we all left this place before we get in trouble."

One by one, the college head coaches spoke briefly to me as they walked out of Henry's Barbeque and headed to their next destinations. Coach Ford was the very last head coach to say his goodbyes, leaving me by myself at the back table of Henry's Barbeque. Before Coach Ford walked out of Henry's, I yelled to him, "Where are you headed now?"

Coach Ford stopped, turned around and said, "They have a big lineman in Kershaw that sure has caught my eye. I'll be there for a few hours tomorrow before I head back to Clemp-son."

As soon as Coach Ford walked away, a young waitress came from the back with a mop and a bucket. As she started to mop the pool of Coach Ford's tobacco spit off the concrete floor, Henry Bozzard came running from the front of the restaurant yelling, "What in the hell are you doing?"

The young waitress replied, "Cleaning up this mess."

Henry cried out, "Are you crazy? That's Danny Ford's spit. Don't you ever touch that. For God's sake, girl, that stain on the floor will be the most famous stain ever made in Coosawhatchie. Danny Ford made that stain and it will stay there forever."

I smiled, threw a couple of dollars on the table and began to walk out. Henry shouted, "Hey, Coach, the next time all of those big-name coaches come through, please let me know so I can be prepared. This is the most business we have had in a long time."

"It won't be any time soon. Thank you and goodnight."

As I walked past an old cigarette vending machine, sitting next to the main entrance, I heard a voice from behind me say, "Hold up, Coach Blake."

When I turned, I immediately recognized the assistant coach from Virginia Tech I met earlier at practice. He said, "I'm Coach Treadway from Virginia—"

"I remember. You're the one who was looking for the liquor store."

Coach Treadway smiled while replying, "I told you I was asking for Coach Fulmer from Tennessee, but after the day you have had, it looks like you could use a stiff drink."

"I usually don't drink during the week, but this has been a long day."

Coach Treadway laughed momentarily before saying, "Well, if you would like a drink, Coach Fulmer left a nice bottle of Old Crow in my car. I'd be glad to share his stash. Ever since I became the Defensive Coordinator at Virginia Tech there have been a couple of times I needed a drink or two,"

I smiled as we walked to Coach Treadway's rental car. I then asked, "You're the defensive coordinator at Virginia Tech? That sounds like such a cool job."

"It's a cool job until Coach Dooley comes on the head sets and threatens to fire you if you don't stop a team from getting a first down on fourth and one."

Coach Treadway opened the driver's side door of his rental car. He then said, "Let me move some of this crap out of the front seat so you can take a load off. I'll tell you all you need to know about college coaching."

For the next forty-five minutes I listened as the Veteran of Vietnam told me about his amazing career that started as an assistant at a small high school in South Carolina called Pageland. I knew exactly where he was talking about. When Coach Treadway told me that coaching college football was all about hard work and lucky breaks, I believed him. Coach Treadway said, "Believe me when I say this, the best teams have the best players. That's why Coach Dooley always tells us something Coach Paterno shared with him a long time ago. He tells us that recruiting is our job. Coaching football is our hobby."

I took a swig from a pint bottle of Old Crow; something I had never done in my life. I began choking and momentarily coughed a few times. I then began laughing when Coach Treadway said, "Hold on, Partner... That Old Crow will fly all over you."

I replied, "That stuff is God awful."

"Tell me about it. I don't know how Coach Fulmer does it." Coach Treadway paused for a moment before saying, "Phil would kill me if he knew I was dogging him so bad. I've known him for a long time, and I can't ever remember him or Coach Majors taking a drink on the recruiting trail. They are both considered some of the good guys in this business and they are always first class."

While we talked, I began to dig deeper into the mindset of a college football coach. I took the opportunity to ask, "Where did you learn all that you need to know about the game of football to coach at your level?"

Coach Treadway smiled, took a swig of Old Crow and said, "I hate to tell you this, but all of us win our battles at places like Henry's Barbeque or in the home of a recruit where we end up eating some undercooked casserole or a piece of stale homemade pie. Saturdays in college football are won from those trips to bum F... Egypt. These are the trips when you have to convince mama, daddy, and grandma that we'll take care of little Johnny better than the other guy. I've been to the slums of Philadelphia and inside houses with no air conditioning or running water. I have traveled to the backwoods of Mississippi as well as the urban jungles of Memphis and Baltimore. Everybody thinks college coaching is so glamorous, but I'm here to tell you that nobody knows anything about all the butt kissing that takes place. Sometimes I wake up in the middle of the night and absolutely have a panic attack. It may be from something simple like forgetting to write a recruit or his parents a thank you note. Then there are times when I have forgotten to pack for a flight to a small school in the middle of nowhere."

I interrupted him and said, "Yes, sir. You're here, right in the middle of nowhere." I then paused and asked Coach Treadway, "So why do you do it?"

"It's all about the competition. As a recruiter, you miss out on about sixty percent of those you chase. Half of this silly game we call recruiting is about throwing off the competition. If you can't sign a kid, part of your job is to block your biggest competition. For example, if I know one hundred percent that Frankie is not going to sign with us, I sure as hell don't want him to sign with our rival, the University of Virginia. But Coach, when you do land a big-time recruit, there is no other feeling in the world that compares. When that kid finally signs on the dotted line there is a feeling of jubilation that I can't describe." He then paused before saying with a serious look on his face, "Don't get me wrong, I love the game of football, but the pressure cooker of college football recruiting drives some men to do things they should never do. You've got to be careful."

"What do you mean?"

Coach Treadway replied, "Don't be surprised if over the next few months a few of these coaches promise you things that they can't deliver. I've seen it all. One day someone will try to slip you a couple hundred dollars, and you will think they really care about you. Some will try to take you out on the town; you will be impressed. Then somebody will offer you a job at their school and you will think that your career is about to take off. Let me warn you, I have seen coaches like you that have crashed and burned when they became too involved with all of the recruiting shenanigans. You look like a nice young man, but let's be honest. You're a black man. Those coaches here tonight see that more than you think. They believe that you have the inside track when it comes to the soul of Frankie Lake. When the circus finally leaves this town, those coaches tonight won't give a flying flip about you or anybody else here. Trust me when I tell you this."

"Thanks, Coach, for all the good advice. I better head to the house. Where are you going tonight?"

Coach Treadway put down the bottle of Old Crow, before saying, "I'll be staying at the Howard Johnson's off I-95."

"Where will you be heading in the morning?"

Coach Treadway smiled before saying, "A little place called Coosawhatchie. I'm here for the rest of the week. Coach Dooley told me that Frankie Lake was his number one priority and put me on the job. I have a feeling that you and I are going to get to know more about each other than we ever imagined.

Chapter Four

The next morning, I received an early phone call at 5:45. In a loud voice, Coach Hanover growled, "You better hustle. Frankie's mama is sick again and he needs a ride to school this morning. It's raining like a SOB so you know the drill."

For me, this wasn't an unusual request because there were many times when Frankie didn't have a ride to school. Frankie lived so far back in the woods that he had to walk over a mile to catch the bus. Rainy days always presented a problem.

When I later turned down the dirt road which led to Frankie's house, I laughed when I had to slowly drive my Ford Tempo through several large puddles on the dirt road. I thought, *driving through the lakes to pick up a Lake.*

I drove by an abandoned barn which appeared to be built at the turn of the century. I always noticed the small junkyard filled with old farm and trucking machinery, including a rusted out combine, rotted tractor tires, and a broken-down flat bed. After finally arriving at a small wooden house which had been the home of Frankie since the day he was born, I blew my horn. I sat parked next to a clump of small pines which looked as poor as the land where they were growing.

Frankie smiled as he jumped in. For the next few minutes we talked about school before Frankie asked, "You thinks we are gonna have a good team next year?"

I shook my head and asked, "What did you think about all of the coaches that came to see you yesterday?"

Frankie rubbed his hands together before saying, "Shoot, Coach... They came to see our team. Coach Hanover always tells me I ain't nothin' without our team."

The more I listened, the more I understood that the superstar of Coosawhatchie was as pure and innocent as a baby lamb. Frankie Lake didn't think what he did on a football field was any more important than what the rest of his teammates did. I tried my best to find out which of the college coaches most impressed him; however, Frankie's only response to my questions was, "They all be nice mens."

I already knew Frankie was a nice kid, but on our way to school that morning, I realized that there wasn't another soul in Coosawhatchie County who was a better human being than Frankie Lake. I quickly understood that Frankie could care less about all the hoopla that surrounded his ability to play football. Before we entered the school parking lot, I asked him, "What would you do with all the money you could make if you made it to the NFL?"

Frankie smiled a big smile before saying, "I'm not sure. I didn't know they paid you to play ball. I guess I woulds plant me a big garden and buys me a puppy."

A few minutes later, I followed Frankie into the main entrance of Coosawhatchie County High School. I almost dropped my briefcase when I saw Coach Treadway, Coach Fulmer, and Coach Kenney standing inside the main lobby. They all stood like statues; dressed in their Virginia Tech, Tennessee, and Penn State coaching shirts. Frankie smiled at them and kept walking to his class. I stopped in front of Coach Treadway and asked, "I didn't think you could contact a recruit during school.

Before he could answer, Coach Fulmer said, "The rules say we can't make contact, but we can speak if the recruit speaks to us."

Coach Treadway stated, "Normally we don't hang around the front office, but today we are all interested in Frankie's transcripts. I think Coach Hanover said he had taken the SAT and ACT earlier in the year. Do you remember what his scores were on those tests? When we asked Coach Hanover he told us that he wasn't sure."

I knew exactly what Frankie made on the tests, but I sidestepped the question fearing it would hurt Frankie's chances of being recruited. I calmly replied, "You would have to ask the people in the front office. I have no idea."

A few minutes later, all three of the assistant college coaches found themselves in a tiny office with Mrs. Shrader. Mrs. Shrader was a longtime fixture at the school who needed to retire years earlier. She practically ran the school, loved the place more than most, and was Coach Hanover's biggest supporter and biggest fan of the Coosawhatchie County High School Crocodiles.

For the next ten minutes she pretended to look in file cabinets for Frankie Lake's test scores. Then when it appeared that the college coaches were getting aggravated, she said, "Lord have mercy, that child's scores have not been sent to us yet. I'll have to call the folks at the College Board and find out why. I know that Frankie told me that he did good."

* * *

Later during my fifth period class, I called Frankie out into the hall. Looking at the star running back I said, "For the rest of the year, I don't want you to do any of the work in my class."

"How come?"

"Because you're going to study for the SAT test coming up next month. If you don't do better on that test, your college career will be put on hold for a while."

I then shoved a large SAT workbook against Frankie's chest and said, "Every day you come to my class, you study this. Every Monday, Tuesday, and Wednesday you grab your lunch and come to my room to go over this book. We have a lot to make up."

Frankie nodded his head and replied, "But I already done took those tests."

I smiled at him saying, “Yes, you did. But you will need to do a little better this time. Now go back into the room and start studying.”

* * *

Football practice that afternoon was a soggy mess as light rain hovered over the area. Coach Hanover changed up the schedule and ordered our coaches to use only rubber balls during practice. We worked on defense the entire time.

The three assistant college coaches patiently watched Frankie make numerous tackles while they caught up on the gossip of their profession. Coach Kenney of Penn State whispered to his colleagues, “Are you two in the hunt for the linebacker from New Jersey? I can’t remember which one of you is after him.”

Coach Fulmer replied, “Heck no. He’s not going to sign with you either. I heard that he was going to Notre Dame whether he wanted to or not.”

Coach Treadway asked, “How do you know that?”

Coach Fulmer pulled up the hood of his orange University of Tennessee rain poncho and replied, “Because his mother told me so on the phone a few days ago. She told me he was going to Notre Dame no matter what.”

Coach Kenney laughed, “Well, there goes another one. I don’t mind telling you guys that I’m in a little bit of a slump right now. If I don’t sign a couple of good recruits this fall, I’m not sure how much longer Coach Paterno is going to be patient with me.”

* * *

After practice ended that afternoon, the three assistant college coaches piled into the office of Coach Hanover to talk football. Coach Hanover always liked to find out about the new strategies the college football coaches were using at their schools. I stood in the corner of the tiny office and listened closely as Coach Treadway explained the Virginia Tech eight-man front blitz package. Writing and erasing on the office chalkboard like a mad scientist college professor teaching advanced students, he was interrupted when Coach Hanover yelled, "Hold on a dang minute. I have no idea what you're talkin' bout. Slow the hell down."

When he dazzled all he could, Coach Treadway threw the piece of chalk to Coach Fulmer of Tennessee and said, "Your turn, big boy."

Coach Fulmer stared at him and said, "No chalk needed. Our offense is pretty simple, but I'll be glad to show you how we would block that garbage Hokie defense you just showed us."

Coach Hanover grumbled, "I know how we'd bust 'em. Block down and kick out. It's that simple."

Coach Kenney interjected, "Yes, sir, I would have to say that Coach Paterno would agree wholeheartedly. At Penn State, we believe everything should be centered around double teams at the point of attack, which in essence becomes nothing more than gap blocking."

Coach Kenney then drew up a couple of running plays on the chalkboard which he said they had been working on at Penn State during their earlier spring practices. When he drew up a fancy bootleg pass, Coach Hanover interrupted, "I appreciate y'all showin' an old dog some new tricks, but here at Coosawhatchie, we is always gonna be simple. Thank you all. It's been fun. Me and Coach Blake have some work to do. We'll see you later."

Once the disappointed looking trio left the office, Coach Hanover looked at me and said, "Sit down. Let's talk."

After I sat down, Coach Hanover stated, "Whenever you have the chance, always pick their brains 'cause at their level, they is all smart, but don't chat too long because you have to remember; they don't give a rat's whisker about you. All they care 'bout is how they can find a way to get what they came for. You should be careful with what you say to these jokers."

* * *

By the end of the week, Spring football practice officially ended at Coosawhatchie County High School. During those last three days of practice, many more college head football coaches visited, hoping to change their program with a young man who was now rumored to be the fastest football player in the nation. The head coaches from Syracuse, NC State, UCLA, LSU, Alabama, Kentucky, Maryland, Iowa, Oklahoma, BYU, Arizona State, Michigan State, Miami, Texas, and Notre Dame had all landed by Thursday and Friday. They landed in either Charleston or Savannah and made their rental car journey along I-95 to the new mecca of recruiting at a little high school in the middle of nowhere. Henry's Barbeque was so busy, he began selling a t-shirt which read: Coosawhatchie- HOME of the LAKE. Henry cooked and sold more hash, rice, baked beans, and pulled pork than ever before. Across at his seafood joint he sold plates of Carolina Crab and named his famous fried seafood platter the "Lake Bake." People from all walks of life came to practice not only to witness the greatness of Frankie Lake, but to also have the opportunity to be close to some of college football's celebrity coaches.

When the previous year's national championship coach, LaVelle Edwards from Brigham Young University came to town, the Principal of Coosawhatchie County High School, Reggie Dean, posed in a picture with him on the front steps of the school along with about fifteen members of his extended family who were all Mormons.

It was purely by coincidence that arch rival coaches Barry Switzer of Oklahoma and Fred Akers of Texas both arrived at Coosawhatchie County High School at the very exact same time. Switzer and his entourage came from the airport in Charleston while Akers and his crowd came via the Savannah airport. The two of them didn't speak to each other until Coach Hanover said, "Ah hell, y'all are in the marshlands far away from that Red River. Y'all can be friends here, and nobody back home will ever know a thing about it."

When the University of Minnesota's Head Football Coach, Lou Holtz came to town, he entertained the crowd at Henry's Barbecue when he performed a few magic card tricks before he explained that he had fond memories of his time as an assistant college football coach at the University of South Carolina. The crowd laughed hysterically when he described how he sold cemetery plots one summer to make extra cash while he lived in Columbia.

I had the pleasure to eat with Coach Holtz and pick the brain of one of college football's most entertaining coaches. He spoke so fast, I had a difficult time hearing all that he said, but when he offered me the chance to work at his summer camp at the University of Minnesota, my heart wanted to say yes, but the words of warning from Coach Treadway and Coach Hanover kept coming to my mind. I declined the fantastic offer and could tell that Coach Holtz didn't like my rejection. I was surprised when our conversation ended when he said, "I can tell by talking to you that you're going to do good in this profession."

He didn't know it, but those kind words from him, made a lasting impression on me that I would never forget.

More people took photographs in Coosawhatchie during that one week than ever before or since. So many autograph and photograph seekers came to town on the last two days of spring practice, Coach Hanover was forced to hold practice at the stadium to accommodate the huge crowd. Never before or since has the stadium at Coosawhatchie been as packed for a practice as it was on Friday afternoon; the last day of spring practice.

Every night that week, I found myself being wined and dined at Henry's Barbeque. I was asked the same questions all while being told I was an incredible young coach. Although I was only twenty-six years old, I was exhausted by the end of the week. I couldn't wait for the circus to leave town. When two different college assistant coaches tried to give me envelopes filled with cash, I was tempted, but I didn't succumb to the temptation. Asked by almost every college program to bring Frankie to their school for summer football camp, one assistant college coach from out West even suggested that he could arrange for me to spend a few days in Las Vegas at the Golden Nugget.

In the midst of the circus atmosphere, Coach Hanover took extra precautions to protect Frankie Lake from being mobbed by coaches and well-wishers. He made all of our assistant coaches escort Frankie from the practice field or the stadium like we were bodyguards. Each afternoon, Coach Hanover personally escorted Frankie out of his office walking him to his pickup truck before he drove his star player home.

Coach Hanover took one more precaution when he made me the permanent personal morning chauffeur of Frankie Lake.

Chapter Five

During the final two weeks of school, the hoopla over Frankie died down in the town, but it didn't die down at the school. Six to eight assistant college football coaches made Coosawhatchie County High School their home away from home. Coach Treadway from Virginia Tech had figured out where I stopped to purchase gas. On the days he was in town, Coach Treadway would miraculously appear at the Crossroads Convenience Store on the way to Frankie's house. At the school, there was no telling where Coach Treadway might end up. One day he was in the cafeteria; then the next day he was reading a newspaper in the school library.

For three straight days, Coach Fulmer from Tennessee would wait to greet me in front of my classroom. He was always sipping a cup of coffee each morning. He was professional and would always tell me that he hated being on the road and away from his family.

The best dressed coach of the trio, Coach Kenney of Penn State made his presence known by wearing an embroidered Penn State tie with his gray tailored suit, a starched white button-down shirt, and fancy Italian shoes. He would only appear during lunch at the school cafeteria. He once told me that college coaching was a full-time 50 weeks out of the year business. By the end of the last day of school, most everyone at Coosawhatchie County High School knew those three coaches like they were a part of the regular school staff.

The mail room at the high school became overwhelmed with literally hundreds of cards, notes, and promotional flyers, from every football college and university in the nation. All of the mail was addressed to Frankie Lake. By the last week of school, the mail lady had to ask me to box up Frankie's mail and take it to the gym. On the last day of school that year, the Postmaster General of the Coosawhatchie post office called the school and requested that they come to the post office to pick up a truckload of Frankie Lake's mail.

After trying to tutor Frankie to prepare him for the SAT test, I finally went to Coach Hanover and said, "There is no way he will ever pass this test. God bless him, but his reading comprehension is very low. Frankie tries like hell, but he is way behind."

Coach Hanover replied, "He will be a Prop 48 or end up at a Junior College in Mississippi. His last scores were the lowest I've ever seen. Maybe he will get lucky, but I'm afraid you may be right."

In between all of the excitement surrounding the star of Coosawhatchie, I began to really learn more about Frankie as a person. I began to learn most everything about his likes and dislikes. One day during lunch when we were going over vocabulary words, Frankie looked up and asked, "Coach, why do people feel the need to use fancy words like - culinary. I don't understand why they just don't say cook or cooking?"

I couldn't help but laugh before saying, "I guess some people want other people to be left in the dark. I really don't know."

Frankie replied, "Maybe the Good Lord decided we could use different words for the same word so life wouldn't be so boring. Whatcha think 'bout that?"

When I asked him if he would like to go to Florida State or Clemson for summer football camp, Frankie said, "Coach, I ain't never been anywhere."

I asked, "What do you mean?"

"I ain't never spent the night nowhere but at my house."

"Get out of here. You mean to tell me that you have never spent the night with a friend or a relative?"

"Not since I was a baby. I don't think I would like the big city. I don't know how to swim, and I ain't ever ate any ice cream."

I asked, "Well, you do know that when you sign with one of these colleges you will have to leave home?"

"Yes, sir, but I don't wants to go until I have to."

"So, let me get this straight. You don't want to go to a camp at one of these colleges this summer?

"No, sir. I have to work this summer to help my Pops."

I eventually learned that Frankie wasn't like the other students I encountered on a daily basis. He wasn't a typical teenager. Frankie knew very little about the real world. His world centered around the pulpwood that his family cut and hauled to the local saw mill which was fifteen miles from his home. He grew up in a house that was heated by a wood burning stove, no air conditioning, and no television. His clothes were washed by hand in a wash tub and most of the food he ate came from the family garden, and the few pigs, chickens, and goats they raised. He and his family attended the Jerusalem Fire Baptized Church whose pastor was the Right Reverend, Dr. Phillip Osborne. The church which was so far out in the country, there were times when they had to cancel services due to rain. The dirt road leading up to the church which sat next to the marsh flooded regularly.

Although most every girl at Coosawhatchie County High School was interested in Frankie, he had no desire to be with any of them in a romantic way. He confided to me that God would provide a wife for him when the time was right. Unlike the other teens his age, Frankie didn't care about the shoes or clothes he wore. He wasn't materialistic and thought that everyone was born with a good heart. I could not believe it when Frankie told me that his favorite songs were "Amazing Grace" and "It is Well."

I asked, "Do you listen to the songs on the radio?"

Franke laughed and said, "Can't say I do. We ain't gots a radio at my house."

"You mean to tell me that you don't listen to Run DMC or the Boogie Boys? How about Lionel Richie?"

Frankie looked at me with a strange look on his face while asking, "Do they sings gospel?"

I shook my head before he also confided that although he struggled academically, he loved being at school because he loved the students and the teachers mainly because of the isolation he experienced living in the backwoods of Coosawhatchie County. Unlike some of the other teenagers that liked to smoke, toke, cuss, and drink alcohol, Frankie had never once participated in these evils.

Each day, I began to dig further trying to find out more about this kid, who by all accounts was an anomaly. Through our further talks, I learned that Frankie's father had been working pulpwood his entire life. James Lake, like Frankie, was tougher than most any man in Coosawhatchie County but he too, had a heart of gold. Unlike Frankie, James never went to school past the fifth grade. The youngest son of the family, James started working at the McClendon Saw Mill when he was twelve years old. He became such a loyal, hard worker, and talented sawyer, Mr. McClendon set him up with an independent trucking contract when he was twenty-four years old. It was a business arrangement that benefited both because James Lake was known as the only person in the county who would venture deep into the local swamps to cut timber. His ability to weave through impassable terrain was legendary. When he later learned how to make bowls, platters, knife handles, spoons, forks, turkey calls, and various knick-knacks from trees he found in the swamp, his woodwork became very sought-after. His perfection of turning a lathe on black walnut, rainbow poplar, rosewood, magnolia, and red oak produced some of the most spectacular works of art in the Lowcountry of South Carolina. Because he sold his works for a lot less than they were worth, he always had more orders than he could physically handle. This production problem led him to rely heavily on his only son, Frankie, to help him with the cutting of pulpwood and the other various chores around the house. He was devoutly religious and believed it was sinful to brag about one's accomplishments. He taught Frankie that the world wasn't a friendly place, but one that needed help and a lot of prayer. His influence on Frankie was forged in the marshlands, swamps, and rivers of their surroundings.

Frankie's mother, Ida Louise, almost died a year after Frankie was born when she was injured by a log that fell off James's truck. Helping her husband near a marsh bog, the log crushed her pelvis and her legs. Four surgeries later, she suffered from the complications of a blood clot to the brain. After her slow and painful recovery, she permanently hobbled along with noticeable slurred speech. She could still manage to drive a car, but only during daylight hours. Frankie loved his mother more than anything and never wanted to disappoint the woman who had taught him to love the nature surrounding his home, never to fight unless it was necessary for survival, and to pray to God every morning before work or school.

I took it upon myself to help Frankie with his speech, grammar, and annunciation problems. Whenever I would hear Frankie use improper English, I would correct him. To my surprise, Frankie listened and tried very hard to do whatever he was being asked. My admiration for Frankie Lake grew as each day passed.

* * *

Before the college coaching circus finally left town for the summer, Coach Treadway made a surprise visit to my rental house on the outskirts of Coosawhatchie on the evening before school ended for summer break. Coach Treadway brushed up against a large azalea bush next to the porch. He almost ripped a big hole his pants when he walked up the steps and knocked on the front door. I was dressed in a pair of sweatpants and an old Citadel t-shirt when I opened the door. I was shocked to see Coach Treadway.

"I know it's late," he said, but I wanted to tell you goodbye before I left in the morning."

For the next hour, I listened to a man whose primary source of income was determined by the number of football recruits he signed for Virginia Tech as well as the number of times he was able to stop the opposition from scoring on Saturday afternoons. After a few minutes of small talk, I asked, "Do you really think you have a chance of landing this kid?"

"You tell me. I'm only doing what my boss tells me to do. I have no idea if Frankie even knows where Virginia Tech is located, much less if we have a chance at him."

I replied, "Good point. I can assure you that he has no idea where your school is located. That young man has only been to Charleston a few times in his life and nowhere else. He is a special young man with a good heart. Wherever he decides to go, he and his family will really have to trust the coaches."

"I'm not sure I know how to gain his trust if I never have the chance to speak to him. You and Coach Hanover have put the barriers up around him the past few weeks."

I shot back, "When all of you coaches ambushed him outside of the locker room on the first day of contact practice, you blew it. Coach Hanover told us that we would be Frankie's bodyguards for the rest of the year."

Coach Treadway stood up on the top step and said, "I hate that." He then shook his head and said, "Believe me when I tell you that the circus is just beginning. This next football season is going to be a lot wilder."

"What do you mean?"

"These college coaches are going to invade this town like nothing you have ever seen. Every Friday night there will be a hoard of coaches at your games. Throw in the official visits to the schools as well as those to Frankie's home, and you guys will be busy trying to watch after Frankie."

I asked, "Will you continue to be a part of the circus?"

Coach Treadway smiled before saying, "As long as Frankie stays undecided, I'll be in this town from August to February at least once or twice a week."

"How many other recruits do you have your sights on?

"Right now, I have three in the Baltimore, DC area that I'm pretty sure will go with us. I also have one in North Carolina and one linebacker in Ocala, Florida who may be tougher than Frankie."

"Do you get tired of the road?"

"I hate flying. I'd rather drive anywhere. That old saying, 'What goes up must come down,' is always in the back of my mind."

We laughed, we talked, and I received an education about time management from a crafty recruiter who wore many hats for Virginia Tech. Before he left that night, Treadway said, "What I do love about this job is meeting people like you. I feel like I now have a friend in Coosawhatchie, South Carolina."

I shook his hand and said, "And I have a friend who resides in Blacksburg, Virginia."

As soon as Coach Treadway drove away, the phone began ringing in my bedroom. I stumbled over a pair of gym shorts and a pair of tennis shoes. I fell on the bed and answered the phone. I was surprised when I heard, "Hey man, this is Coach Ford. I know that tomorrow is the last day of school. What are you going to do this weekend?"

"Well, I don't... have any plans right now."

"Great. My wife, Deborah, is dragging me down to Hilton Head for a couple of days of relaxation. I would love for you to meet my family and have lunch or dinner with us. It's not that far away from Coosawhatchie."

"Coach, thank you, but..."

"But nothing. Pack your swimsuit. We'll have a good time, and I promise we'll not talk about Frankie. I want to get to know you better. I have a feeling that one day I may be coaching against you."

I laughed loud before replying, "I don't ever see that happening."

Coach Ford replied with a serious tone, "You need to have more self-confidence. I'm a pretty good judge of character. It's not hard to see that you're a good coach. The one who needs to know that is you."

After Coach Ford convinced me to make the trip to Hilton Head along with giving me directions, I sat on the side of my bed and began to think about how far I had already come in my young career. I laughed when I thought about my parents who met while my father was stationed in Japan for a tour of duty with the United States Navy. My father, 2nd Lt. Carl Blake, later served in Vietnam while his young family lived in San Diego. My first memories as a child were forged in the California sun with my mother. My teen years were spent in Charleston, South Carolina, where my father ended his notable military career. During my high school years, I excelled in football and track at a private Catholic school in Charleston. When the Citadel offered me a scholarship to play football, my father was ecstatic because he wanted me to serve in the military.

Upon my graduation from the Citadel, I knew I disappointed my supportive parents when I decided I wanted to become a teacher and coach. Long discussions about my career options caused a major rift between my father and me. My father could not believe that his son was graduating from a military college, choosing not to serve in the armed forces. More than anything, I wanted to excel in the coaching profession to make my father proud.

I then thought about my future career goals. Did I really want to continue down the path as a high school teacher and coach or did I want to explore my options and try to enter the college coaching ranks by becoming a graduate assistant or by meeting the right person who could propel my career? I was young, single, and desperately trying to figure it all out in the midst of a recruiting war that I had been placed in by coincidence and sheer luck. A part of me knew that my career could possibly be entering a new phase because of an athletic phenom named Frankie Lake.

Chapter Six

The next morning, the sound of battering on the side of my house had my full attention. It wasn't the first time that a red headed woodpecker had made an early morning attack on some of the rotten pine boards on the side of the house. After fully waking up, I shaved and showered. I then walked into the kitchen and opened the refrigerator finding only a small carton of milk with an expiration date long gone. I packed a swimsuit just in case. I then began watching the morning news on a television channel out of Savannah all the while I wished I had cable so I could watch ESPN.

For the next few minutes I pondered over if I should really show up in Hilton Head to eat lunch with Coach Danny Ford and his family. I was smart enough to know that the only reason I was being invited was because of Frankie Lake, but I was just naive enough to believe that Coach Ford really wanted to get to know me better. Then it occurred to me that no matter what, I would be passing up an opportunity that many football fans would envy if I didn't go. Spending time with one of college football's most famous people convinced me that I needed to go. Right before I turned off the television, the phone in my room began ringing. When I answered it, I couldn't believe another famous voice was on the other end of the line.

"Hey, Coach Blake, this is Coach Schembechler. I hate to bother you this morning, but I wanted to make sure that you knew you were invited to come to our summer camp in a few weeks. Now you know that I can't pay for your flight up here to Ann Arbor, but the money you will make during our one-week camp will make it worth your while."

The famed coach from Michigan then asked about Frankie before ending the conversation. He said, "Even if Frankie decides not come to our camp, I still want you to visit with us."

He talked a few more minutes about the humid weather of the South Carolina Lowcountry. I sidestepped him several more times and didn't give Coach Schembechler a firm commitment about attending his camp. I then hung up the phone, locked the door to my house, cranked up my Ford Tempo, and began driving toward Hilton Head.

My favorite radio station from Savannah played the new hit song, "Freaks Come out Night" by Whodini as I rode into the city limits of Coosawhatchie. While the rap song played loudly in my car, I thought about Frankie never listening to the radio. A few minutes later I came to a stop sign on the edge of town. I turned off the radio and thought back to a conversation I had with Frankie where he confided to me that he had never once had the opportunity to experience the sensation of eating an ice cream cone. I decided at that moment that since it was on my way to Hilton Head and I was in no rush, I would stop at the Coosawhatchie Dairy Queen and take Frankie an ice cream cone. Once inside the small fast food diner, I momentarily hesitated and wondered if it was a good idea to barge in on Franke and his family unannounced. Then a rather large white lady from behind the grill yelled at me. She said, "Technically we ain't open for another thirty minutes, but as long as I don't have to cook anything I can take your order."

"Yes, ma'am. I would like to order one large vanilla ice cream in a cup with a cone on the side."

She yelled, "That will be two 'vanill-er' scoops in a to- go- cup. Throw in a cone."

Since she was the only person in the Dairy Queen, I asked her who she was talking to.

She replied, “That’s how we call out the order up in here even if we are workin’ alone.”

She then looked at me and asked, “Ain't you that coach from the high school that all the little girls talk about when they come up in here?”

Somewhat embarrassed but quite flattered, I replied, “You must have me mistaken for somebody else.”

She grinned before asking me, “Ain’t you the only black coach at the school?”

“Yes, ma’am.”

“Then it’s you. All the black girls and many of the white girls is always up in here talkin’ about how they is in love with you.”

Not knowing how to respond, I smiled as she handed me my ice cream cup and a cone. She then asked, “You married or have a girlfriend?”

“No, ma’am.”

“Watch out! It won’t be long. One of these girls in this town is gonna hook ya before you know it.”

I was about to open my car door when a white Ferrari 400i with a Clemson University license plate on the front, pulled up next to me with its horn honking. I immediately recognized Donald Chafin, one of the richest men in Coosawhatchie County.

He was known all over the Lowcountry of South Carolina as Tiger Don. He had made a fortune in the early 1970s when he landed a lowball bid for a government contract to install all of the drain culverts down the South Carolina portion of Interstate 95 from North Carolina to the Georgia state line. At the time when he secured the contract, Don had recently inherited a small paving company from a childless uncle who killed himself by jumping off the Coosawhatchie River Bridge. Don didn’t possess the first bit of knowledge about construction when the I-95 contract made him an instant millionaire. He hired some good help for the massive construction project and it paid off. A few years later, he struck it rich again when he became the first person in Coosawhatchie County to install a tanning bed salon and a satellite television company.

He was called Tiger Don because he loved the Clemson University Tigers so much. Everything he owned was colored either orange, white, or purple. His swimming pool was made in the shape of a Clemson Tiger Paw logo. His mansion stuck out like a sore thumb because every bit of it was painted orange. Every person in Coosawhatchie County knew they were passing his property one half mile before they arrived because he had worked out a deal with the South Carolina Highway Commissioner to allow that stretch of the county highway to have orange Clemson logo tiger paws painted on it every fifty feet. Tiger Don never attended a college or a university but grew up loving the Clemson Tigers.

Tiger Don put his Ferrari in park, jumped out and yelled, “Good mornin, Coach Blake. I saw you comin’ out of the DQ and I wanted to ask you how things were goin’ with our boy?”

“Which boy are you talking about?”

The darkly tanned robust Tiger Don smiled as he replied, “Frankie Lake, of course. I just want you and B.B. to know that if Frankie ever wants to take a ride up to Clemson, I have a little place up there on Lake Hartwell where he or any of you coaches can stay.”

I didn’t know what to say, but quickly thanked him for his kind offer. I badly wanted to tell him that I was going to visit Coach Danny Ford, but I knew if I did, I would never get away from the most fanatical Clemson football fan I had ever met.

About twenty minutes later, I was driving down the dirt road which led to Frankie Lake’s house. Almost a half a mile before I reached the house, I saw a white, 1983 Pontiac with dealer tags on it parked on the side of the road almost in the ditch. When I finally made it to Frankie’s house I was able to see Frankie and his father, James talking to another black man dressed in a red and gray colored jumpsuit and a pair of shiny white tennis shoes. The black man wearing sunglasses smiled at me when I parked and began walking toward the house. They were all sitting on the front porch when I said, "I hope I'm not disturbing you, but I wanted to drop this off."

Frankie looked at his father and said, "This is Coach Blake who picks me up in the mornings."

James Lake stood up, walked down the steps of the porch before saying, "I need to thank you, Coach Blake. I've heard a lot 'bout you. You comin' by to pick Frankie up has been a blessin' to us. What you have in that sack?"

"I thought Frankie would like to try some ice cream. He told me he had never eaten ice cream before."

James Lake shook his head saying, "That's mighty nice of you, but Frankie don't eat much sugar or sweets here. When Frankie turns twenty-one he can eat whatever he wants, but for right now in this house, he eats what we provide."

I could tell that James Lake wasn't very happy about the ice cream, but he wasn't disrespectful. James then turned toward the porch before asking, "Do you two know each other?"

Before I could reply, the young-looking black man wearing a jumpsuit stood up from his chair on the porch and said, "I don't think we have. I'm Coach Jaden Geiger. I'm a graduate assistant coach at the University of South Carolina."

He then walked down the steps and shook my hand.

I was aggravated when I asked, "I didn't think you coaches could visit a recruit's home like this without it being an official visit?"

Coach Geiger smiled before saying, "Oh no, Coach. This is not an official visit. My car seems to have run out of gas on my way to Savannah. I was all turned around with my directions. The next thing you know, I'm out here in the country looking for a gas station. I had no idea that these nice people would be willing to help me out. And come to find out, Frankie is being recruited by our school. Now that's quite a coincidence, wouldn't you say?"

I gave Coach Geiger a long stare before saying, "Well, you know the rules. You best be on your way. I'll drive you to the gas station and help you with your gas. I'm sure Mr. Lake has an empty gas container we can borrow."

James Lake spoke up saying, "We already put the gas in his car. Coach Geiger is gonna eat some lunch with us before he heads on out. You're more than welcome to stay as well."

I respectfully declined the offer but before I left, I said, "Coach Geiger, I would like to have a word with you before I go."

He looked at me kind of funny and then replied, "Sure, no problem."

As the two of us walked toward my car, I whispered, "I know what you're doing. Who do you think you are?"

Coach Geiger whispered back, "You better get one thing clear, nobody is going to stop me from signing this boy. Do you know what it will mean for my career if I can get him to commit to the University of South Carolina? Now help a brother out and keep quiet about this. I can't believe you decided to show up on a Saturday morning."

Although my blood was boiling, I calmly replied, "Now you get this straight. I'm not your brother. Frankie Lake is a special kid. I'll do whatever I have to do to protect him. Do you understand?"

Coach Geiger laughed for a few seconds and then said, "If you can help me sign this kid, it will help both of us. You think about it. There is so much good we could accomplish if we work together on this situation."

I shook my head before saying, "I don't want anything to do with that. Now eat quickly and leave, or I'll tell my boss what has happened. I know for a fact you don't want Coach Hanover calling your boss, Coach Morrison."

* * *

I then began driving down the backroads and through the marshlands toward Hilton Head. I was furious about what I had stumbled onto. I began to wonder how many other coaches had ventured into the marsh to the home of Frankie Lake. I desperately wanted to call Coach Hanover or tell Coach Danny Ford about what had occurred. A few miles later, I decided against it. I thought about the face of Coach Geiger. I was giving him the benefit of the doubt because he was a young black man not much younger than me. I knew Coach Geiger was trying to make a name for himself in a profession dominated by white men.

As I later crossed the bridge into Hilton Head, I had only a few memories of the place where I once played a high school football game in the upscale town developed for people who had a lot more money than I could dream about. Driving by the expensive beach homes, golf courses, and the yachts of Harbor Town, I felt like I was in territory where I wasn't welcome. At the first stoplight, I noticed an older white man looking over at me from the inside of his Pontiac. When I glanced in his direction, I could see that he was staring at me with a frown on his face. I felt awkward. I was about to flip him off when suddenly he motioned for me to roll down my car window. While I rolled down the window, several bad thoughts crossed my mind. The older man then yelled through his car window saying, "I graduated from the Citadel in 1939. Nice car, young man."

I then realized he had seen my Citadel Football sticker that was on my back bumper. I was embarrassed that I had prejudged him as I waved goodbye.

I thought about several things as I came to one of Hilton Head's many traffic circles. Confused momentarily, I immediately knew I had taken a wrong turn. I made a U-turn a block later. I then pulled into the parking lot of a dry cleaners so I could look more closely at the directions given to me by Coach Ford.

Several miles later I drove up to a large beachfront property called the Sea Castle. Before I could cut off my car engine, I could see Coach Danny Ford walking toward me from the steps of a large beach house. Coach Ford, wearing an orange Clemson baseball cap, a Hawaiian looking shirt, black Clemson gym shorts, and flip flops, had a big chaw of tobacco in his mouth. He yelled at me, "I'm so glad you decided to join us. I hope you like hamburgers and hot dogs. Nothing fancy at this place."

Before I could reply, Coach Ford was attacked by his two oldest daughters, eleven-year-old Jennifer and nine-year-old Ashley. They both tried to jump on the back of their father. Coach Ford introduced them to me and said, "These wild girls have been running me ragged down the beach this morning. We are making up for some lost time."

Inside of the lavishly furnished beach home, Coach Ford confided to me that a Clemson University football booster allowed him and his wife to stay there a few times during the year. He then whispered to me that the beach wasn't really his cup of tea, but his girls loved it. Coach Ford's wife, Deborah then walked into the den of the beach house holding their three-year-old daughter, Elizabeth. Deborah looked a lot younger than I expected. She introduced herself and her daughter by saying, "Look here, Elizabeth, this is the coach who told your daddy to get his lazy b-hind off the practice field."

I felt embarrassed. I quickly replied, "I didn't..."

Deborah interrupted me by laughing before saying, "I know. Danny told me all about it, but he did say that your diplomacy regarding the situation was impressive. He also told me that he wished he could have taken a picture of your face when you gave him the message."

"Yes, ma'am."

Deborah then bent over and allowed Elizabeth to walk over to her father. She then said, "Coach Blake, this is the newest addition to our family. I have an idea that she is going to be her Daddy's little Tomboy. She follows Danny all over the farm back in Clemson."

Coach Ford picked up his youngest daughter while saying, "Stephen, you need to find a good woman like Deborah. I don't know what I would do without her."

Deborah laughed and said, "I can tell Danny is almost beached out after one day. He has been playing with the girls on the beach all morning. They made some impressive sandcastles while I laid out and read a novel that came out last year called the *Wasp Factory* by Iain Banks. It was a little too gruesome for my taste."

She then apologized to me for what they were serving for lunch. She said, "The girls have been begging their Daddy to grill some hot dogs and hamburgers. Stephen, I hope you weren't expecting anything fancy."

During our lunch, I was surprised that the couple, who met each other while attending high school in Gadsden, Alabama, never once mentioned Frankie Lake or recruiting. I was also surprised that they ate off paper plates with only a big bag of potato chips as the side dish. To me, the Fords' acted like real people who treated me like I was just another member of their family.

As we continued our conversation, Deborah stated, "Danny is like a big bear with his claws missing. He growls a lot, but he is one big teddy bear."

Coach Ford looked at me while saying, "She has me pegged pretty good. It seems like yesterday she begged me to marry her."

The girls along with Deborah all began to giggle while the oldest daughter, Jennifer cried out, "Daddy is such a liar. He is the one who asked Mama to marry him."

Two hotdogs later, I wished that I could have recorded our conversations. I could not believe I was eating and conversing with one of the most sought-after head coaches in college football and his wife. The more we talked, I realized that Danny Ford and his wife were more than celebrities; they were down to earth people who really didn't care about fame and fortune. They both told me how fortunate they had been during Danny's young career while they highlighted the lucky breaks along his career path. Then surprisingly, they both confided that the last two years had been tough because the Clemson football program was put on probation by the NCAA for recruiting violations. Deborah said, "The only substantial violation they could find was when Danny paid a dental bill for one of his players to have a cracked tooth fixed. They did a lot of digging to find out that my husband did what any other good-hearted person would have done in the same situation."

Coach Ford added, "Four years ago I was on top of the world after we won the National Championship, and then we were hit with the probation almost a year later. Let me tell you, that part of my job has not been fun."

Coach Ford then surprised me when he asked me to tell them my personal story about my family and my career. As I rambled I noticed that they both seemed like they were really interested in what I had to say. Then after about fifteen minutes, Deborah suddenly pointed over at nine-year-old Ashley who was dozing off at the table. Deborah said, "Excuse me, Stephen. It looks like it's nap time for the Ford girls."

While she ushered the girls to the back bedroom, Coach Ford stood up and said, "Come out here on this amazing back porch. The view of the ocean is incredible."

After Coach Ford talked briefly about the shoreline of Hilton Head, he began talking about his days as a player for Coach Bear Bryant at the University of Alabama. He said, "Coach Bryant was as tough as they come, but I learned so much from him that had nothing to do with football. I cried like a baby the day he died. The man was more than a football coach to me; he was a teacher of life lessons. I tried to emulate everything he did well as a coach while adding my own philosophy. I knew I had to be Danny and not the Bear."

I then leaned over on the bannister of the porch and asked, "Coach Ford, why did you ask me to come over here today?"

Coach Ford stood back away from the bannister and sat down in a rocking chair. He then replied, "I told you that I wanted to get to know you better. I know what you're thinkin'. Well, let me tell you, there is no doubt that you would not be here today if it wasn't for Frankie Lake being a part of your life, but you being here right now has more to do with the way you interacted with me while I was in Coosawhatchie."

"What do you mean?"

The youngest coach to ever win a NCAA College Football Championship simply replied, "Because I can tell you're good people."

I raised my voice saying, "There has to be more to it than that."

Coach Ford replied, "I want you to know that I think you're already a good coach. I saw how you reacted to your players and how they reacted to you. It was fun to watch you at practice the other day. Then the way you handled yourself in that barbeque joint was admirable. All of us head coaches really put you on the spot, but you delivered. Now you know I can't offer you a job at Clemp-son, but I sure do know a lot of people in this state when you decide to make a move from Coosawhatchie. I know what you're thinkin,' but I promise on my grandmother's grave that I don't want anything in return. Sure, the competitive side of me wants that Lake kid to sign with us, but you being here today has nothing to do with that. One day, this state is going to have many more black coaches as opportunities once not heard of become available. Times are changing in the South and all over this country. I think you should have the opportunity that has not been afforded to others in your same situation. I grew up in Alabama where I saw firsthand the ugliness of racism. I want all that to change; particularly in my profession. I haven't met too many young black coaches like you, and I want to help."

I didn't know how to respond. I knew that a lot of what Coach Ford was saying made sense, but I could still not believe that Coach Danny Ford wanted to personally help me with my career. I loved the attention I was receiving; however, I took it all with a feeling of nervous trepidation. Before I could respond, Coach Ford and I both heard the ringing of the doorbell.

A few seconds later, Deborah came to the sliding glass door which led to the back porch. She opened the door and said, "Danny, Miles is here."

"Tell him to come out here."

When the man came out on the porch, Coach Ford looked at me and said, "Stephen, I want you to meet Coach Miles Aldridge. We just hired him. I wanted Coach Aldridge to meet you because he will be the one in charge of recruiting Frankie from our staff. Coosawhatchie is in his recruiting territory."

The thirty-four-year-old blond coach looked like he could have been a surfer or a professional wrestler in his younger days. His looks reminded me of the actor, Nick Nolte. With a Marlboro cigarette hanging from his bottom lip, Coach Aldridge walked over to me and shook my hand before saying, "Coach Ford tells me there is a special kid in your neck of the woods. I can't wait to meet him this coming year."

"He is really special."

Aldridge quickly asked, "I hear he is struggling with his test scores. Do you think that's going to be a problem?"

"He has been working hard. I have to believe he will do much better this time." I then paused before asking, "How did you know his test scores?"

Coach Aldridge replied, "Because it's my job to know everything so that we don't get caught by any surprises."

Coach Ford interrupted the conversation saying, "That's enough of the business talk. Coach Aldridge wants to take us to do a little surf fishing. I hope you'll join us. Miles knows everything there is to know about sea fishin'. Me, on the other hand - I'm a freshwater pond kind of fisherman. I love to catch the bream and the big bass."

I was briefly tempted but replied, "No, sir, I appreciate the offer, but I have a date back in Coosawhatchie. If I stand her up again, I might as well call it quits."

Coach Ford smiled and said, "She sounds special."

I smiled back at him and said, "She could be."

Ford looked at Aldridge and said, "Sounds like fishin' with us is out of the question. Coach Blake has a mermaid waitin' on him back home."

Aldridge said, "You can't blame him for that. If I had a mermaid waiting for me, I wouldn't be fishing either."

Coach Ford then turned toward me and pulled out a business card from his wallet while saying, "Anytime you need to talk to me, you give me a call. On the back of the card you will find my home phone number."

I took the card and put it in my wallet before saying, "Thanks, Coach. It's not hard to see why so many players love playing for you."

Chapter Seven

Something seemed a little fishy to me as I began driving back to Coosawhatchie. I desperately wanted to believe everything I had been told by Coach Ford, however when Coach Aldridge arrived, the timing of his arrival seemed staged and rather odd. I then thought it would be uncanny if Coach Aldridge had driven all the way from Clemson to Hilton Head to do a little fishing with his boss. It didn't seem to add up.

As I continued to drive through the marshlands, I then pondered over my career as well as a young lady named Shahrazad Shirani. She was my Saturday night date. I then thought about the ingredients that I needed for the dinner I promised her I would make.

I had recently met the first-year middle school math teacher a few weeks before at a school district meeting arranged through the College of Charleston. The informational meeting was for teachers who were interested in obtaining their Master's in Secondary School Administration; a requirement for any teacher who wanted to enter the administrative side of education. After the meeting, it was by accident that I was able to meet Shahrazad when her car's battery went dead. Once I was able to determine her battery was shot, I did what any gentleman would do and offered her a ride. That short ride across town turned into a long conversation where I learned that one of the most beautiful women I had ever met was a transplant from New Jersey. She informed me that after trying in vain to secure employment in New Jersey as a teacher after her college graduation, she secured a job in Coosawhatchie in a state education system that desperately needed math teachers. She was the daughter of two Iranian college students who came to the

United States in 1958 to study the arts. Shahrazad, who went by 'Shah," grew up in a home filled with the belief that each person should work hard and pursue their own destiny.

On that first encounter Shah laughed at my Southern accent even though I didn't think I had one at all. I laughed at the way she whined when she voiced her words in a Jersey accent that was undeniable. The only thing Iranian about her was her beautiful Persian complexion and shiny dark black hair. Her personality and demeanor was no accident because her parents wanted her to become as Americanized as possible.

Because of spring football practice and the college coaching hoopla over Frankie Lake, Shah and I didn't have any free time to go on our first official date. Two cancellations and several phone calls later, she finally agreed to allow me to cook her dinner at my place. In my mind I was way out of my league. In her mind, she worried that by having dinner at my place, I would think she was being too forward. Without too many places to go on a Saturday night in Coosawhatchie, she reluctantly accepted my invitation because she was bored out of her mind. Coosawhatchie wasn't anything like where she had grown up in Jersey City.

That evening when Shah arrived, the first thing she noticed was the aroma of a Lowcountry boil. The Zatarain based spices from my signature dish permeated my entire house. I greeted her with a formal hug which seemed awkward to both of us. With the television playing an episode of the series, *Different Strokes,* Shah laughed and pointed toward the television screen. She said in a deep voice, "What you talking about, Willis?"

I laughed before saying, "Arnold cracks me up. Come into the kitchen, and let's eat."

After I poured us a glass of moderately expensive red wine, I held up my glass and said, "To friendship in the middle of small-town South Carolina."

Shah toasted with me and replied, "I would have never dreamed that I would end up in Coosawhatchie after I graduated from Rutgers, but you have to admit that this place kind of grows on you after a while."

After trying a few bites of my Lowcountry boil, Shah looked at me and said, "Where did you find this sausage? It's outstanding, and the shrimp, well, they are out of this world."

After dinner that evening we shared our thoughts on many subjects along with our personal hopes and dreams. She explained that she loved helping disadvantaged students. I shared with her my concerns regarding the recruitment of Frankie Lake. By the time *Saturday Night Live* came on television, we had learned more about each other than we expected, and fell for one another in an unexpected way. A girl from New Jersey, who grew up in a semi-practicing Muslim home, and a young coach from Charleston, who was raised Catholic and graduated from a military college somehow found a special connection in the middle of nowhere.

* * *

For the next two weeks of summer vacation, Shah and I spent as much time with each other as possible. We took day trips to Savannah, Beaufort, and Charleston. We visited the ruins of the Old Sheldon Church, near Beaufort which was built in 1745. I even gave her a tour of my college alma mater, The Citadel. We took a couple of picnics near Coosawhatchie and even went to the beach at Sullivan's Island for a day.

Those two weeks were the most enjoyable times of our young lives. Unfortunately, one day when we were walking through the old Charleston City Market on Meeting Street, we stopped at a table filled with antique coins and Confederate paper bills. The lady who was selling the historical items was very pleasant, but an older white man with a cane, who had followed us, kept staring at Shah and I finally asked him, "Is there a problem?"

His stare could have killed. He then said, "You two should be ashamed of yourselves."

I quickly asked, "Why do you say that, sir?"

"Whites and Blacks ain't supposed to be with each other."

Shah reacted instantly. "That's really funny. For your ignorant information, I'm Persian, not White. Besides, who made you so powerful that you can judge people you don't even know?"

The old white man tried to respond, but before he could say a word, Shah verbally blasted him again. "It must be horrible having so much hate in your soul. You're an old man, and if I were you, I would lose the hate before your last day arrives."

The old man would not stop; neither would Shah. Finally, at the boiling point of the heated exchange, I had to forcefully pull Shah away, thinking she was going to kill the old man with his own cane.

A few minutes later as we continued to walk through the Market, we both realized that our relationship would be something that not everyone agreed with. We didn't talk about it, but we knew. At that moment, I reflected back to my high school days when I was one of a few African Americans at my school. I remembered the looks of horror on the faces of white parents whenever one of their daughters would talk to me after a game or at a class activity. I had lived in Charleston, and I learned early that there were many people who publicly supported and liked me as long as I didn't date their daughter. My parents and I had many conversations about the unwritten rules of society. Whenever I was around my white friends, the topic was seldom talked about. My black friends and I talked about race a lot. It was a topic that was always in the back of my mind.

By the time I was attending the Citadel, I knew that the subject of interracial dating and marriage was something not everyone I encountered felt comfortable with. I was always careful regarding that subject.

This particular encounter bothered Shah deeply. She had never experienced someone being vocal about their prejudices. She couldn't believe that I was calm during the episode with the rude man. I then explained to her that I had experienced similar situations on more than one occasion during my teen years.

Much later that afternoon, we stood on the Battery in Charleston near Rainbow Row, I kissed my new love, and told her that I loved her.

"I'm so happy to hear that because I love you too."

As we spent more time together we learned about our quirks, likes, and dislikes. We shared our dreams and talked to each other like best friends. She learned that I had been raised in a family that valued education above almost everything else. Being raised in a military family, I was exposed to many different people and different cultures. In my mind, I wasn't what many had labeled as a stereotypical black man. She agreed.

I also learned that Shah too, had been raised in a family that placed a high priority on education. Although her parents were Muslim, they openly accepted others of different faiths and ethnicity. They taught Shah to be an independent woman who accepted others based on their actions; not by some preconceived beliefs or prejudices.

* * *

During those two weeks of summer vacation, Coach Hanover was busy spending his time pulling irrigation hoses and sprinklers across the Coosawhatchie Stadium turf in the morning and cutting the grass in the afternoons. Almost every evening, he drove out to Frankie Lake's home to help him prepare for the upcoming SAT test. Tired and sweaty from a hard day's work, Frankie could barely concentrate while he and Coach Hanover went over vocabulary words and worked on math problem examples from a study guide. When they were about to wrap up their last study session, Frankie surprised Coach Hanover when he asked, "What do you think is the most important thing in life, Coach?"

Hanover thought for a few seconds and replied, "That's a loaded question, but I would have to say that service to others has to be right there at the top of my list. Money, fortune, and fame all come and go. I believe we were put on this planet to serve others."

James Lake, who was sitting in a chair not far from them, heard their conversation. He smiled, and said, "Amen, Coach. That's what I'm talkin' bout."

* * *

On June 13, 1985, there was nobody in the town of Coosawhatchie prouder of Frankie Lake than Coach Hanover when Frankie entered the high school that morning to take his second SAT examination. No one knew it, but Coach Hanover prayed silently that Frankie would prevail.

Around lunchtime when many of the other students had finished with the timed examination, Frankie and four other students were still taking the exam because a substitute from out of town showed up late when a regularly scheduled teacher called in sick. An hour and a half after most of the other students had finished, Frankie Lake walked up to the substitute teacher, thanked him, and turned in the most important exam of his life. When he walked out of Coosawhatchie County High School he was greeted by Coach Hanover and several reporters who wanted to know how he did. Frankie smiled and told the members of the media, "Piece of cakes."

* * *

Unlike other high schools in South Carolina, pre-season football strength and conditioning workouts didn't start in Coosawhatchie until after the 4th of July. Coach Hanover who grew up in the town, never tried to have workouts in June because he knew better. His players had to work during the summer. While other schools held their summer strength and conditioning workouts in the mornings, Coach Hanover held his workouts from 8pm to 9:30 pm because all of the players on his teams worked during daylight hours.

The day the team assembled together for the first time on the evening of July 6th, Coach Hanover had received some really good news. He shared it with the team when he yelled, "Got good news. Frankie done passed the SAT!"

As the team roared and clapped for Frankie, I whispered to another assistant coach, "I can't believe it."

After Coach Hanover showed his assistant coaches Frankie's score of 1190, I shook my head in disbelief. According to that piece of green paper, Frankie Lake was now not only academically eligible to play football at a college or university; he was eligible for the schools with the highest academic standards.

A few days later when his scores became the topic of conversation in the college football coaching world, some of the elite academic institutions of the nation began to throw their hat into the ring. The head coaches at Duke, Stanford, Georgia Tech, Wake Forest, and Vanderbilt all began dreaming about the one recruit who could impact their football program more than any other.

By the end of July, the Postmaster of Coosawhatchie had to hire another part-time worker to keep up with the mail for Frankie Lake. Frankie's passing test scores also served as an economic catalyst for the town of Coosawhatchie as many of the national media descended on the town to write or broadcast stories surrounding the nation's top football prospect. Henry Bozzard and several other local entrepreneurs were rolling in the dough with every new customer that walked into their establishments. When Henry began to sell bottles of what he called 'Lake Water,' regional merchants jumped all over the chance to sell water that supposedly made a person faster. The two gas stations in Coosawhatchie began selling more gas than ever before while the

Tidewater Bay Motel, the only accommodations available inside the city limits, saw their first new customers in years. At the Coosawhatchie Dairy Queen, posters of Frankie were being sold so fast, the printer in Charleston could not keep up. The business of Frankie Lake was booming except for the fact that Frankie Lake wasn't receiving a dime for the use of his name, his likeness, or image.

This injustice didn't go unnoticed by Coach Hanover. We both warned the local business leaders that Frankie needed some kind of compensation for their economic success. When Henry Bozzard told Hanover that Frankie and his family could eat free anytime they wanted, Hanover became agitated. He yelled at Henry, "A few plates of pork and hash ain't gonna cut it, partner. Y'all keep on, and all of y'all are gonna start a Civil War in this town."

When the owner of the Dairy Queen offered to give me a handful of free milkshake coupons to give to Frankie, I laughed at him and said, "You know that's not nearly enough."

The Civil War of Coosawhatchie could have been avoided, but not after the Reverend Dr. Phillip Osborne of the Jerusalem Fire Baptized Church became involved. That was the spark that caused the eruption.

Two weeks before the first practice in August, a media frenzy occurred on the steps of the Coosawhatchie Courthouse when Dr. Osborne held a press conference with Frankie Lake and James Lake by his side. After claiming that the local merchants were exploiting the talented teenager, Dr. Osborne introduced an attorney from Charleston named Eli Burroughs. Eli was a firebrand attorney who had already become famous for representing numerous clients in high-profile Civil Rights cases all over the South. The mere mention of his name in some towns caused business owners to settle long before he took them to court. He was loud. He was brash. He was what every person of color needed when he represented them over various legal matters. Smarter than what some of his supporters called a "dumb country fox," Eli was the NAACP's best legal mind in South Carolina. He had won, he had won big, and he kept winning.

On that scorching mid-summer day in July, when he came forward to the makeshift podium on the Coosawhatchie Courthouse steps, most of the crowd of black citizens clapped loudly while most of the town's white residents stood silent. Eli put his arm around the neck of Frankie Lake and said, "There will be no peace in this town until my client is properly compensated." He then took a deep breath and cried out, "If any of you think you can hoodoo my client out of this compensation, then you're in for a long legal battle."

Chapter Eight

Some of the old people in Coosawhatchie best described the hot humid July's of the area as the smell of hell. If you could smell the unique aroma of the marshlands in July, according to legend, you were close to hell, in hell, or going to hell. It all depended on how bad the marsh smelled to a particular individual.

The idea of hell crossed my mind a couple of times late that summer when the other assistant football coaches at Coosawhatchie County High School and I melted under the heat and humidity of July. Coach Hanover made all of the assistant coaches clean out the grass and weeds which had grown on the clay track that surrounded the football stadium field. It was an annual tradition that had been done for years. Coaches armed with hoes, rakes, and shovels, worked for one week in the blistering heat to rid the orangish colored red clay track of various weeds, Bermuda and Bahia grasses. When one coach suggested that they spray the track with diesel fuel, Coach Hanover cried out, "That diesel might seep onto the game field."

One of the beleaguered coaches rolled his eyes before saying, "So what. At least we'll be alive to see it."

On the last day of raking and ridding the track of its botanical nemeses, Coach Hanover brought all of his coaches Coca Colas on ice and moon pies he had purchased at the Crossroads Country Store. While we sat under the home side of the stadium bleachers seeking relief from the brutal Carolina sun and humidity, Coach Hanover shouted at us, "I 'preciate y'all's hard work. Lord knows I wish I could pay you more. I want ya to know- this year is gonna be special. I can feel it in my soul."

While we had been working to get rid of the weeds on the stadium track, Henry Bozzard was working with his attorney to figure out a good defense for a possible legal battle with Civil Rights attorney Eli Burroughs and the NAACP. Eating a pulled pork plate, his attorney, Derwin D. Dorman, from Hilton Head, wiped his mouth with his napkin and said, "They don't have a legal precedent to collect one dime from you; however, you might want to throw some cash at the Lake kid in a good faith effort to hush this thing up before it turns ugly."

Unbeknownst to them at the time, back in the marshlands at the Jerusalem Fire Baptized Church, what Reverend Osborne and a group of his supporters were planning was something that was unthinkable. He and a few of the older men of the community had been persuaded by Eli Burroughs that if the white businessmen of the community would not pay up, then football season at Coosawhatchie County High School would be played without the participation of the African American players. They began arranging for a boycott of the season and a march right down Main Street. When they excluded Coach Hanover from these discussions, they made a critical error because the African American players and many of their parents trusted Coach Hanover more than they did a lawyer from Charleston and a preacher who had a small flock in the backwoods smack in the middle of nowhere.

When James Lake heard what they were proposing, he too, didn't like what he was hearing. He wanted Frankie to play ball.

Three phone calls later that evening, Coach Hanover was well aware of what was about to occur. One phone call later, he summoned me to meet him at the school to discuss the situation. After hanging up the phone and agreeing to meet him, I called Shah and briefly explained the crisis to her. After hearing what I had to say, she said, "I certainly hope that you're going to support the boycott."

"Are you kidding me? If all those players don't play, the season is doomed."

"Oh, you mean to tell me that you of all people support those white business owners who have exploited this poor young man?"

"Hell no, but I can tell you that if Frankie and those players don't play, nothing good will come out of this. He and several other of our players can kiss their scholarship dreams goodbye."

The news concerning a possible boycott of football season traveled fast that night in Coosawhatchie. For the first time since the public schools were integrated, race became the main topic of conversation. Tensions were high on both sides of the debate. Everyone in town had an opinion, and some people on both sides said some ugly things that they would later regret. In a town where most everyone seemed to get along, people who cared for each other for an entire lifetime were now reluctant to be seen together. In only a few short days, it seemed that years of racial reconciliation and harmony had been destroyed.

Coach Hanover, who had worked all his life to right the wrongs from the past, was having none of it. When it was announced that the Committee for Racial Justice was meeting the next night at the Jerusalem Fire Baptized Church, Coach Hanover picked me up and we headed there without a formal invitation. On our ride over, Coach Hanover glanced at me and said, "I'll be danged if these clowns are gonna ruin this season. I done worked too hard for this mess to end somethin' special. And damn, that's what this season is gonna be, something really special."

I didn't comment because I was somewhat offended. Although I didn't agree with the boycott of the football season, I did think the black citizens and Frankie Lake had a legitimate gripe. I didn't think anyone was a clown. I then began to question if Coach Hanover took me along only because I was black. Before we entered the overflow church that evening, I mustered up enough courage to ask him, "Did you bring me here because I'm black?"

"Hell no. I brought you here tonight because you're Frankie's position coach. I can't help it if you happen to be a black man."

A few minutes later, I was astonished by the reaction of many of the people in the church when Hanover and I walked inside. As I followed Coach Hanover down to the front of the church, I noticed that many of the people in attendance lowered their heads not looking at Coach Hanover. Whether they did it out of hate, shame, fear, or respect, I can't say, but it was sure noticeable.

When Coach Hanover made it all the way to the altar of the church, Eli Burroughs was preaching loudly. He cried out, "Now is the time for action."

As the already famous Civil Rights attorney continued to rile up the crowd, Coach Hanover did a most peculiar thing as he knelt down on the first step of the church altar and began praying silently. I was standing next to him. I didn't know what to do. I thought to myself that if I kept standing beside Coach Hanover it would appear that I was acting as a bodyguard for the only white man in the building. If I knelt down with him, it would appear that I was trying to be religious during a serious discussion that didn't need to mix religion with politics. Before I could decide what was best to do, Eli Burroughs pointed his finger at Coach Hanover and said, "All these white men like this one don't want anything but your money."

After he said those words, most of the people in the church gasped and some of them actually cried out, "Lord Have Mercy! Say it ain't so...Say it ain't so!"

Coach Hanover stood up and walked up the steps toward the podium. He looked like a wild boar in the marsh when he approached the podium. Nobody knew if he was going to punch out the Civil Rights attorney from Charleston or if he was going to offer some kind of spiritual words of wisdom. Without a word, Dr. Osborne pulled Eli Burroughs away from the podium and allowed Hanover to speak.

Coach Hanover wiped his forehead with a handkerchief before saying, "I know most of y'all and before I say what I came to say, if anyone in this church thinks I don't care about the black chil'ren of this community, tell me to my face right now."

The people sat in silence for a few seconds until one lady in the back of the church yelled out, "We know ya love us, Coach. We know ya love us."

While some of the people in the church began to laugh, Coach Hanover laughed along with them. He then looked out over the crowd and said, "Don't do this. You have every right to be mad with the business owners, but you don't have the right to be mad at me or OUR boys who have worked so hard to bring another championship back to Coosawhatchie County. If you want to boycott, go right ahead and boycott those businesses, but don't ruin this special season because you're mad.

"You all know that I fought in Korea and that I saw some ugly things, things I don't want ever to talk about. My prayer tonight is for peace, peace in my hometown."

After he said those words, everyone in the church stood up and gave him a standing ovation. Even those who didn't agree with his plea to leave the football program out of the boycott applauded Coach Hanover because he was the only white person in town who openly seemed to care about the injustice. While he and I walked out down the main aisle of the church, I could not believe the handshakes and hugs for a man who was an enigma to many in the community. I knew that this outpouring of emotions were heartfelt expressions of love for a man they knew cared about them.

For some reason I wasn't convinced that his efforts were all honorable. I questioned his motives. I wasn't sure if he was only concerned about the upcoming season. While we drove past a large moss-covered oak a quarter of a mile past the Jerusalem Fire Baptized Church, I asked my boss, "There's something that's bothering me, and I need to know the answer. Did you hire me because I'm a black man?"

He pulled over his old Chevy truck on the side of the dirt road. He looked at me with a frown on his face and said, "After workin' with me for two years, I hope that you know me better than that. What I'm about to tell you is somethin' I don't share with many folks, but you need to hear it. I hope you will appreciate what I'm about to tell you."

He then rolled down his window and explained that when he was serving in Korea, he saw some of the most horrible things you could ever imagine. He didn't know it at the time, but his battalion was fighting for a hill that held important strategic value. He and his fellow soldiers called it Suicide Hill because of the number of men that were killed when they tried to advance. By chance, he had met a young corporal who was named Donte' Davis. He was a black man not much younger than Hanover, who was serving in an all-black unit. Coach Hanover's platoon was segregated at the time. One night, before they were engaged with the enemy, he and Donte' met when Donte' was sent to ask Hanover about ammunition. During their conversation, Coach Hanover learned that Donte' was from a small town in South Georgia called Willacoochee.

Immediately, before they found themselves fighting for a piece of Korean real-estate, Hanover nicknamed, Donte,' "Mr. Willacoochee" because he thought the name of his hometown was as unusual as his.

A few nights later, before they were about to enter battle, Coach Hanover had the opportunity to speak with Mr. Willacoochee once again, when Donte' was asking him privately about their next morning battle plans. Hanover loved Donte's personality and his fighting spirit. He said that Donte' wasn't scared of anything.

As they talked that night, Coach Hanover learned that Donte' and his family were poor like his. Donte' talked about some of the food he missed from back home in Willacoochee; some of the same food Coach Hanover was also missing. They laughed about how only a few people they had encountered in Korea appreciated a good pot of grits or a slab of cornbread dipped in the juice of collards they both called "pot licka." Hanover still remembered Donte' telling him that he thought it was ironic that two poor rascals from towns that had strange names, ended up in Korea fighting in a place that nobody would ever remember. Donte' joked that Hanover's hometown of Coosawhatchie sounded a whole lot more country than Willacoochee.

Before they ended their conversation, Donte' wanted him to know that he was fighting for more than saving the country from the communists. He wanted things to change back home after the war for he and his fellow black brothers and sisters. In a charismatic way of expression, Donte' told Coach Hanover that if black and white folks could fight together in battle, they sure as hell ought to be able to live with each other during peaceful times. Donte' then talked about respect and equal rights. He made Coach Hanover realize that things back home between whites and blacks needed to change. Donte' may have been poor, but according to Hanover, he was well-read and seemed to be well educated. Donte' then worried about going home after the war. He explained to Coach Hanover, the beating of Sergeant Isaac Woodard, Jr.; a beating that left the honorably discharged soldier from World War II, blind when he was dragged off a bus in South Carolina for no reason and beaten by the local police. Donte' further explained that the Woodard incident is what caused President Harry Truman to integrate the military in 1948.

Donte' said, "Here we are in Korea supposed to be integrated and look around. By the order of the President, we are supposed to be equal, but I don't see it happening. That's what worries me."

The more Hanover listened to Donte,' the more he agreed with him. Although neither of them knew it at the time, their conversation that night made a lasting impression on Hanover. The next day when Donte' was killed in action, his dying words to Hanover near the base of Suicide Hill, never left his soul.

"While I held his hand on the battlefield, Corporal Donte' Davis from Willacoochee, Georgia, a true American hero, said to me, 'When you finally make it back to Coosa-Hatchie, don't you ever forget that Mr. Willacoochee fought like hell, loved his family more than they ever knew, and died on this damn hill knowing that we all may look different, speak different, and have different beliefs, but in the end, what matters most is that we all bleed red. If people could understand that we are really all the same, this world would be so much better and there would be no more fightin' like here at Suicide Hill.'

"My new friend lost his life that day, and a few hours later, I almost lost mine. When I was blessed to survive and come back home, I never forgot what Mr. Willacoochee told me. So, to answer your question, the answer is not a simple yes and no. Yes, I hired you because you're a black man. No, I didn't hire you just because you're a black man. The main reason I hired you was because our young men, both black and white, need to see a role model like you. They see all the negative things about young black men portrayed in the media; they need to see someone like you in real life, who dispels the old myths about young black men not being able to be successful. I did my homework on you before I hired you.

"One thing you can be damn sure of is that if I didn't think you could coach, you would have never been hired. As much as I always wanted a black coach on my staff, I assure you that I have passed on several black coaches through the years that I thought were not capable of being a good coach. Believe me when I tell you that when it comes to coachin' football, I'll never hire someone out of pity. Stephen, I think one of the most important things that has made me a successful head coach, is that I have a pretty good track record on the people I have hired. Up to this point, you have done nothin' but prove that I hired the best coach possible. You bein' a black coach is an added bonus for our young men and our community."

That night after our talk, my mind changed about Coach Hanover. Much later that evening, the crowd inside of the church overwhelmingly voted to boycott the white businesses of Coosawhatchie; however, they flatly rejected any notion that African American football players boycott the season.

* * *

The next Monday, two weeks before school started in Coosawhatchie, the first official football practice of the fall season was scheduled to take place that evening. By the time the practice started, the town of Coosawhatchie had turned into a media circus. The Committee for Racial Justice along with almost every black citizen in the county, marched down Main Street from the Crossroads Country Store to the steps of the Coosawhatchie Courthouse early that morning. News crews, writers, and journalists from Charleston and Savannah along with national media crews came in droves hoping to cover the biggest news event in the county since a few years back a trailer truck loaded with live turkeys flipped over on I-95, killing all the turkeys and halting northbound traffic. Secretly, many members of the media were hoping that there would be chaos, violence, and bloodshed. One journalist from Savannah told one of his colleagues, "Fightin' in the streets sells newspapers. I hope like hell these rascals have a dang throwdown."

Some of his colleagues, who agreed with his philosophy, went as far as to interview marchers and non-marchers, trying all they could do to persuade them into starting a ruckus or a riot.

The celebrity that all of the members of the news media had come to see that day didn't show up. Frankie and James Lake were deep in a swamp cutting timber that morning. Reverend Osborne and attorney Eli Burroughs were not happy, but they led the march anyway. Most noticeable in the crowd of marchers that morning was the man in the rear of the marchers whose presence offered peace in a town that could have exploded into hatred and violence. When some of the poor and middle-class white people noticed Coach Hanover marching in support of the boycott, some of them joined him. When some of the black protesters noticed that Coach Hanover was leading a small unplanned army of white citizens into their protest, they ushered the coach through the middle of the crowd. After several of our black football players realized their head coach was there in support, they enthusiastically approached him with smiles, handshakes, high fives, and a few hugs. I was amazed by the reaction of the people. I followed my boss not believing how well he was being accepted.

By the time we reached the Courthouse steps without any violence or counter protests, Eli Burroughs wasn't happy to see Coach Hanover standing at the front of the crowd. When a news reporter from a Charleston television station recognized Coach Hanover, the reporter raced over to him with his cameraman. With a microphone and television camera shoved near his face, the reporter asked, "Coach, where is Frankie Lake?"

Coach Hanover replied, "I have no idea."

The reporter kept needling him by asking, "Did you forbid him from showing up today?"

"No, I didn't."

"Are you here today to keep the black players of Coosawhatchie County High School from boycotting football season?"

"No more comments. I'm here to support the citizens of my hometown."

Later that evening when the local news station from Charleston aired their story about the protest, Coach Hanover's comment was taken out of context. The news station inadvertently cut off his full response, only airing his reply, "No more comments."

For the people in Charleston who saw the news clip that evening, his response was meaningless; however, for the black citizens in Coosawhatchie County that news clip changed everything. It now seemed to them that Coach Hanover was only interested in saving a football season.

When the news aired at 6 p.m. that evening, it sent shockwaves through the county. Most of the black citizens were convinced Coach Hanover had ordered Frankie Lake not to attend the protest, and they believed that Hanover's presence at the protest was for his personal gain. Many of the white citizens believed he was a fake who wanted to save a season while playing both sides of the local controversy. Coach Hanover, the man who had served his community for years was now being discredited by one news clip.

Neither Coach Hanover or I ever saw the news clip that afternoon when players began to arriving at the school for the first official practice. Young men who had been working most of the afternoon came into the locker room looking filthy and dirty from a hard day's work. A few of them were eating bites of sandwiches or chips as they changed out of their work clothes. While the coaches were handing out equipment and mouthpieces, a fight broke out in the locker room between one white player and one black player. It was unusual and it was loud. By the time the players were separated, tensions were extremely high. Coach Hanover blew his whistle and ordered all of the players into the gym. Filing into the gym, a few players could be heard mumbling under their breath. Coach Hanover yelled out, "I un warned ya once. Da hammer done come."

The man perceived as the God of Coosawhatchie County football stood in front of his team ready to get to the bottom of the foolishness that had taken place in his locker room. Suddenly before he began to speak a black, freshman, football player stood up and said, "We heard what you said on the news today. I for one am not going to play ball this year."

Coach Hanover was stunned. He had no idea what the young man was talking about. In all his years as the head football coach, he had never once had a player stand up and speak his mind to the entire team without his permission. All of us were in a state of shock because a freshman had been bold enough to speak his mind.

Coach Hanover sensing that his team was on the brink of a full mutiny replied back to the player, "Germaine, I have no idea 'bout what you're talkin' 'bout but you not playin' football is not the answer to the problems we face in this town."

Germaine Mazyck calmly replied, "Maybe so, but after what you said on television, my mama said I can't play for you."

When several other of the players clapped for their teammate, Coach Hanover asked, "What in the hell are you talkin' bout?"

After Germaine explained why he was so upset, Coach Hanover did his best to correct the statement that was taken out of context by a news outlet in Charleston. The conversation became heated when Frankie Lake stood up and said, "Coach ain't against us. He loves us."

A white player named Jeff Sims shouted, "You need to shut the hell up. You're the one who has caused all this mess in our town."

I yelled, "All of you need to calm down. Frankie had nothing to do with this. As a matter of fact, he wasn't even at the protest today."

Germaine cried, "That's because Coach Hanover told him not to be there."

Frankie yelled, "No, he did not. Me and my Pops had to work."

* * *

Practice that evening at Coosawhatchie County High School was one of the most horrible things I had ever witnessed as a coach. Some of the players who participated in football for the love of the game, were not sure if they wanted to play or not. Minus eight key black players including Germaine Mazyck and three white starters including Jeff Sims, the fortunes of a championship season didn't appear to be possible. On his way out of the gym that evening before practice, Jeff Sims yelled at Coach Hanover, "You're tryin' to ruin my Daddy's business. He ain't got nothin' to do with this mess and his business is being boycotted. He ain't been nothin' but nice to every black customer that has ever come into his laundromat. Thanks, Coach. My Daddy said you can go straight to hell."

I, and the other assistant coaches were worried about our boss at the end of practice when Coach Hanover gave a tearful and emotional plea to his team to put aside their differences and work together. Even when he said, "We all bleed green," the remaining players on the team outfitted with dark green practice jerseys didn't want to listen to what he had to say. His demeanor and his stature all seemed to take on a new personification. He was a man who appeared whipped and emotionally drained. Nobody in Coosawhatchie had ever seen Coach B.B. look so bad. Nobody would ever know how his soul was being crushed.

Chapter Nine

Much later that evening, I tried my best to calm down my new girlfriend, Shah, who wanted me to boycott the football season. She explained that I could be a shining example to the other black players and their families. I explained to her that boycotting a football season was out of the question for more than personal reasons. Our conversation became even more heated when she said that she heard one woman in town call me an "Uncle Tom." By the time she left my house I wasn't sure what direction our relationship was heading.

Before I sat down and turned on the television, I pulled out my wallet and placed it on an antique looking coffee table sitting next to my small couch. The wallet flopped open and I could clearly see a white business card which had a Clemson University logo of a tiger paw printed in orange. I pulled out the card and remembered that Coach Danny Ford had given me the card a few weeks earlier. I then looked at my wristwatch. It was almost eleven. I hesitated for a few seconds before deciding to pick up the phone. A few seconds later while I lay on my bed, I gave the famous coach from Clemson University a call at his residence. Three rings later, I almost hung up the phone before I heard, "Hello. This is Danny."

I paused momentarily before saying, "Coach Ford, this is Coach Blake in Coosawhatchie. I sure do hate that I'm calling this late but, we sure could use your help."

Coach Ford patiently listened to me explain what was happening in Coosawhatchie. He then said, "You mean to tell me that Henry Bozzard has stirred up this hornet's nest?"

"Do you know Henry?"

"You bet. He's one of the biggest football boosters for Clempson in the Lowcountry. Don't you worry, Coach, if I have to come down there and kick Henry's Whatcha ma call it...I'll deal with Henry tonight. Let me go so I can give him a piece of my mind."

I never heard exactly what Coach Ford told Henry Bozzard that evening, but whatever it was, Henry Bozzard had a radical change of heart. The next afternoon the local news media once again descended on Coosawhatchie to attend a quickly arranged news conference on the front steps of Henry's Barbeque Restaurant. The jovial owner of a restaurant and fireworks empire, stood in front of the cameras and apologized for the 'big misunderstanding' that had taken place in his hometown. He cried out, "I have in my hand a check for ten thousand dollars that will be put into a special account for Frankie Lake once he finishes his college career."

One news reporter yelled out, "Why not give him the money, now?"

"Because that would be against the rules of the NCAA. That money will be waitin' on him when he is through with his education."

Another reporter asked, "What changed your mind about this?"

"Let's just say that I prayed about it and saw the light. We are so proud of this young man and want nothin' but the best for he and his family."

* * *

Later that afternoon, all of the players who had walked out on Coach Hanover showed up to the Coosawhatchie County High School Gym to apologize to their coach because in essence the Civil War was over. They all wanted back on the team. When Coach Hanover told them that they would have to pay a little hell for creating a lot of hell, he hugged each of them and said, "Y'all get dressed so we can practice."

When I told Coach Hanover about my phone conversation with Danny Ford, he thanked me before saying, "A lot of these people down here love Danny Ford. Remind me to thank him the next time he comes here to visit."

I nodded yes and then replied, "And if he wants to lay on a blocking dummy on the practice field, you better leave that man alone."

* * *

Practice that night seemed like old times. It was impressive. Coach Hanover told me, "I ain't even gonna run 'em. We look like we could beat the Atlanta Falcons. I ain't ever seen a defense that looked so good."

Then in an instant, Coach Hanover fell to the ground like he had been shot in the back of the head. Before the ambulance could arrive, the sixty-one-year-old coach had turned three different shades of purple. Some of the other assistant coaches and myself performed CPR. We did our best to revive our boss. While I gave Coach Hanover mouth to mouth, several of the players wanted to gag. We all thought Coach Hanover was a dead man when he rode off in the ambulance with sirens blaring.

Four hours later, in a hospital in Savannah, we found out Coach Hanover was still alive. He underwent emergency surgery for a bad heart that was blocked to capacity. The cardiologist of the Savannah Christian Hospital told Mrs. Hanover and her grown daughter that their husband and father had made it through the three-hour surgery, but that he was still not out of the woods. The doctor stated, "He's a tough rascal, but his heart is as bad as I have ever seen."

Paige Hanover, the toughest coach's wife in the state of South Carolina replied, "My husband will surprise the hell out of everybody. He'll be back to normal before you know it."

I then heard the Principal of Coosawhatchie County High School, Reggie Dean, speaking to Paige in the waiting room. "I've already decided we'll cancel practice for the rest of the week until we find out more about Coach Hanover's condition. This will also give us some time so we can put something in place if Coach Hanover has to stay here longer than a few days."

Paige Hanover shouted, "Have you lost your mind? No, sir, those boys need to practice. My husband would want them to practice. He has all the faith in Coach Blake so go ahead right now and name him the interim head coach until my husband returns."

I had only briefly spoken to Paige Hanover a few times since I arrived in Coosawhatchie. I couldn't believe her pronouncement. Principal Dean looked at me and whispered, "You heard what the lady said. Starting right now, you're in charge of our football program. Don't screw it up."

Early that morning as I drove back from Savannah, a part of me was excited about the opportunity to showcase my skills as a temporary head football coach. Then as I crossed the Savannah River into South Carolina, my thoughts of glory and career advancement evaporated into the marsh. Reality hit me hard when I thought about the implications of a black man in charge of the football program in Coosawhatchie. I wasn't sure that the other assistant coaches or the vast majority of people in town were ready for such a thing to happen. I wanted to show everyone what I could do; however, I didn't want my efforts to be ridiculed more harshly than others because of my race. For a few moments I lamented over the obvious. Then my Citadel military training along with my father's military influence kicked in. My mind raced as I thought about all the things that needed to be accomplished. I had watched Coach Hanover for two years do things I questioned. I had also watched Coach Hanover be successful when others thought it was impossible. I then began to ponder over the little things that made him a success. Most importantly above everything else, I realized that he had made the game of football simple, easy to understand, without complication or expectations that were unrealistic. He also cared deeply about his players. He was tough on his players; however, his players knew that he genuinely cared for them; he had established relationships with them that would last long after they graduated.

As I watched the sun rise through the shadows of the swamps near Coosawhatchie, I made the decision to keep everything about the program the same. I would not deviate from a plan which had produced more winning seasons than all of the players had been alive. As far as I was concerned, whenever someone came to see Coosawhatchie play football for the next few weeks they would assume that Coach Hanover was sitting in the stands calling all the shots.

Three hours of sleep later, I was woken by Shah knocking on my door. At first, I didn't want to let her in, thinking she was there to continue an earlier argument that had gone unresolved. Several knocks later, I finally opened the door. Before I could say a word, she reached for me and began hugging me with all of her might. She began crying. I held her tight for almost a minute before asking, "What's wrong?"

She fought back her tears and replied, "I'm sorry for making you feel so bad. I hope you know that I love you."

Once I explained that Coach Hanover had suffered a heart attack and that I had been at the hospital all night, she held me tighter. For the next hour I told her all that I knew, including my immediate promotion as the interim head football coach at Coosawhatchie County High School.

She held my hand and said, "You can do this. You're prepared. This community needs you to be strong. I want you to know that you can count on me to be here for you. I have missed you and thought you didn't love me anymore. Please forgive me."

Once forgiveness had been granted, we ate from a warmed-up plate of leftovers. We talked for a few more minutes before I told her that I had to go. I then kissed her goodbye and headed to the school to make plans for the evening practice.

* * *

Inside the small coaches' office, I realized that I didn't have a key to Coach Hanover's office. For a few minutes I thought about calling Principal Dean to ask him for a key. I then realized that Coach Hanover's office was sacred ground that I didn't need to disturb. I quickly made the executive decision that football operations at Coosawhatchie County High School would not encroach into the office of the man, who had built a football empire; without his expressed consent.

Although two of the older assistant coaches were not happy about me being placed in charge, none of them objected to my face. Everyone involved with the program knew that the most important thing at the time was to show the players that nothing had really changed. During the staff meeting before practice, I said, "We'll act like Coach Hanover will be back in a few days. Agreed?"

The four other assistant coaches were all in agreement.

During another spectacular practice, I yelled at my running backs, saying, "I un told ya once. I tell ya again, and the hammer done come."

Frankie and the rest of the running backs began laughing. Frankie said, "Coach Blake, you can't say it like Coach Hanover. You don't scare us like he does."

With a twelve-play scrimmage planned at the end of practice, the defense whipped the offensive scout team so badly, I ended it after only six plays. I told one of the assistant coaches, "Somebody on that offensive side is going to get hurt if we continue."

We finished practice that night with six rounds of Coach Hanover's favorite drill, the 'Sidewinder.' As the players jumped over the cotton rows, many of them yelled out, "We can't be beat! "Then on the last sets of sprints and jumps they all yelled a favorite verse from the school's fight song, "Coosa - Coosa- Who? Coosawhatchie, Coosawhatchie, Fight, Fight, Fight."

At the end of practice, Frankie Lake asked me if he could speak to the team. I spoke to the team first, saying, "Frankie wants to talk to us."

Franke stood up and said, "Take off y'all's helmets and bow y'all's heads." Once the entire team became silent, Franke cried out. "Lord be with Coach Hanover. Let him know we loves him and miss him. Amen."

* * *

Early the next morning, I received a phone call from Paige Hanover. She said, "I wanted you to know that my old cuss of a husband is doing much better this morning. His doctor thinks he will be out of here in a few weeks. He has no idea if he will be able to come back and coach. That will take some time."

"I see."

"He is still out of it most of the time, but when I told him that you were in charge of the team, he smiled." She then paused and continued, "You may not know this, but my husband thinks the world of you. He doesn't tell people those kinds of things so I thought you would like to know."

"Thank you, Mrs. Hanover. I'll keep you and Coach in my prayers."

"And I'll keep you in my prayers because I know how these people can be.... Well, let's just say, win and everything will be fine."

Her phone call motivated me to work harder than I had ever worked in my life. The last thing I wanted was to let down Coach Hanover as well as the entire town of Coosawhatchie.

Chapter Ten

With the Civil War now over in Coosawhatchie and the first week of the school year officially underway without incident, the first few preseason football practices went as smoothly as possible. What changed for many in the small town was that the college football coaching circus came back bigger than before. The other assistant coaches and I did our best to keep the college coaches away from Frankie Lake, but it was becoming almost impossible with so many of them entering the building. The usual trio of Coach Treadway, Coach Fulmer, and Coach Kenney were now joined by graduate assistant coach Jaden Geiger from the University of South Carolina, and Coach Miles Aldridge from Clemson University. They and about six to fifteen other college assistant coaches a day made visiting Coosawhatchie County High School a priority in their recruiting efforts.

Aldridge thought he was making some progress one morning when Frankie walked by several other college coaches but decided to stop and tell him good morning. When he later noticed that Frankie sat down in the cafeteria with Jaden Geiger from the University of South Carolina, Aldridge was visibly upset. He told Treadway, "I'm afraid he's making a connection with the Lake kid that we can't make."

Fulmer said, "South Carolina and Coach Morrison have a good strategy playing out down here. Every other day or two they send another assistant coach to visit while keeping this young graduate assistant coming back and forth from here to Columbia on a daily basis. If you think about it, it's a good strategy."

Kenney clapped his hands softly before saying, "That may be true, but I have to believe that when all said and done, this kid will bolt out of this state. I have heard from a good source that his father wants him to sign with someone out of state."

Treadway smiled and said, "Not only that, my sources tell me that he wants his son to be close to West Virginia because they have cousins living there."

Aldridge shook his head and said, "You're both crazy. None of us stand a chance if that young coach from South Carolina stays down here. Look over there at them laughing with each other. They look like best friends."

That night after practice, the 'friendship' continued as Coach Geiger was seen with Frankie Lake and several of the players of our team eating at Henry's Barbeque. When Henry Bozzard noticed what was taking place, he made a phone call to me. Fifteen minutes later, I walked into Henry's Barbeque with a bad attitude. Henry met me near the counter and whispered, "That coach from South Carolina has Frankie and several of those boys listenin' to every word he is sayin'. You have to end this right now."

I didn't trust Henry as far as I could throw him. I asked, "What does all of this have to do with you?"

"I don't think it's a secret that I love Clemson almost more than I do my own wife. I'll be danged if I'm going to let that coach from South Carolina have a free meal ticket in my joint. No, sir, I want Frankie Lake to sign with Clemson and Coach Danny Ford. I can't stand the University of South Carolina."

Once I entered the main area of the restaurant, Coach Geiger excused himself from the table of teenagers and walked over to me. He said, "I know what you're thinking, but I was already here when they approached me. I swear I didn't approach them."

"How did they know you would be here? Frankie never comes here to eat."

Coach Geiger replied, "I really don't know. I guess Frankie may have heard me asking another student which place served the best food in town. I swear I didn't plan this."

I didn't want to make a scene so I simply said, "Goodbye."

As I watched Geiger pay for his meal and leave, Henry walked over to me and said, "I'll give him one thing; he is one slick dude... You need to do a better job of keepin' him away from Frankie."

* * *

Saturday morning came crashing into my bedroom bringing bright rays of Carolina sunshine that slipped through the blinds enough to wake me up. I covered my head with my pillow two times before I decided that sleep wasn't an option. A few minutes later while I put a pot of water on the stove for my morning coffee, I heard someone knocking at my door. Standing outside on my porch was the Sheriff from Coosawhatchie County, Hank Varnadore and two of his deputies. I opened the door and asked, "What seems to be the problem so early in the morning?"

Sheriff Varnadore, a four-time elected official of the county, whose father and grandfather had been the only men ever elected as Sheriff in the past one hundred years, looked very serious when he asked, "Can we come in and chat with ya?"

I answered yes, but I thought the worst about my parents, Shah, or Coach Hanover. I expected the worst, but I didn't expect what Sheriff Varnadore said. The old, bald headed, darkly tanned, thirty-three-year veteran of Lowcountry law enforcement, asked, "When was the last time you saw Coach Jaden Geiger?"

"Last night around 9 o'clock at Henry's Barbeque. Why do you ask?"

The Sheriff pulled out a can of Skoal tobacco and threw in a large pinch into his mouth before replying, "Cause early this morning, the Highway Patrol found his rental car in the edge of Daisy Creek next to a cypress stump with all the car doors opened wide, and the engine still runnin'."

I asked, "Where is Coach Geiger?"

"We were hopin' that you might know the answer to that question. We assumed he may have been drunk and abandoned his car and maybe someone he knew picked him up. The way it looks right now, we suspect foul play. The dogs didn't pick up his scent, and there aren't any tracks into the swamp. I'm afraid he has vanished into thin air."

After questioning me further, I told the Sheriff about the verbal confrontation I had with Coach Geiger at Henry's Barbeque; the same story he had already heard from other witnesses.

Sheriff Varnadore said, "I don't mind tellin' you that the news media has already gotten wind of all this. Hell, Governor Riley is one step away from callin' out the National Guard and the FBI. I didn't know it, but the Governor is a graduate of the University of South Carolina, and he wants answers as to where this coach has gone off to."

I spoke up saying, "I wish I knew. The last time I saw him, he was walking out of the restaurant."

* * *

By that afternoon, the investigation into the disappearance of Coach Geiger had made regional and national news. Volunteers from all over the Lowcountry came from small towns like Yemassee, and as far away as Orangeburg to search for the man who vanished next to Daisy Creek. Some brought boats and some brought four wheelers. They looked in the swamps, and they knocked on doors. They looked in hog pens, chicken coops, and old barns near Daisy Creek. They went deep into the swamps and marshlands yelling out his name. Divers from the Department of Wildlife searched the deepest parts of Daisy Creek and found nothing. Frankie Lake and his father James even helped out in the search. It seemed that the entire town of Coosawhatchie was looking for Coach Geiger while praying that he would be found alive.

Sunday morning, investigators received a tip that wasn't expected from a most unreliable witness. Slick Davenport, a homeless man, who slept under the Coosawhatchie Bridge off I-

95, claimed he saw three white men wearing white hoods tackle a black man in the parking lot of the Pine Needle Motor Court next to the Interstate. He told authorities that he had been digging in the dumpster outside the motel when the men piled out of a dark colored minivan, held the black man at gunpoint, handcuffed him, and scooped him into the van. One of the hooded men then jumped into Coach Geiger's car and they left at the same time. Authorities concluded that Slick may have been a little drunk at the time, but his eyewitness testimony matched because that was the exact motel where Coach Geiger was registered.

The news media lost their minds over this new revelation and immediately concluded that the Ku Klux Klan was involved in this possible kidnapping or murder. The headlines of most papers across the region read: Klan Abducts Black Coach."

* * *

Law enforcement helicopters and hundreds of bloodhounds went on a wild goose chase all over Coosawhatchie County. FBI agents from Washington DC worked hand-in-hand with local authorities to find the missing coach. Journalists wrote new stories every day while billboards from Savannah all the way to South of Border near the North Carolina state line were put up with a picture of Coach Geiger and a direct hotline phone number to the FBI. University of South Carolina Head Football Coach Joe Morrison held a news conference on the steps of the South Carolina State House with Governor Dick Riley by his side. Coach Morrison pleaded with the public to come forward with any information regarding the disappearance of his young coach.

Although tragic, the business of search and rescue brought another economic boom to the business community of Coosawhatchie. News reporters along with investigators from as far away as Texas descended on the town looking for clues, eyewitnesses, and any scoop related to the case. Sensational news stories came out of Coosawhatchie County every day for a national audience who seemed thirsty for any news about the Klan or Coach Geiger. Henry Bozzard stuck his business fingers into the action as he sold fifty cent buttons of a picture of Coach Geiger with a yellow ribbon and a caption which read; Come Home Coach Geiger. Every known former felon, and anyone ever considered to have any association or knowledge of the Ku Klux Klan was questioned, watched, and investigated. Not a word.

When a reward in the amount of twenty thousand dollars for any information regarding the whereabouts of Coach Geiger was announced to the public a few weeks later, the FBI hotline was bombarded by phone calls as far away as Daytona, Florida. Anyone who had seen a dark colored van called the hotline and gave the location of where and when they had seen such a van. In all, there were over five hundred supposed sightings of a dark van in a geographical area that stretched over one hundred square miles. Every owner of a dark colored van in two counties was found, questioned, and had to offer an alibi to the authorities. On top of the van sighting calls, many people took it upon themselves to accuse a suspicious neighbor, work colleague, or relative; hoping their hunch would lead to them receiving a nice jackpot. A thousand phone calls later, the FBI and local law enforcement spent days chasing leads which never produced any results.

* * *

While the town of Coosawhatchie was making national news, Coach Hanover was slowly progressing from a massive heart attack in the Savannah Christian Hospital. Two weeks after his heart attack, Shah and I were allowed to visit the legend of Coosawhatchie. We were surprised to find Coach Hanover sitting up in a chair when we walked into his hospital room. Even more surprising to us were the number of flowers, cards, and care baskets which filled the room. I couldn't help but notice the cards from the various colleges and universities which were all in the recruiting battle for Frankie Lake. Before we could speak, Coach

Hanover said, "You two must be bored out of your mind to come here to see me. I ain't no better than crab bait right now."

I laughed at him before saying, "Shah made me come and visit with you. I told her that you probably needed more rest."

"The hell with rest. We have a big game this week against Nixville. They ain't ever much to look at, but I know Coach Barnes will have them ready. The most important question is, are we ready?"

"We look as good as any team you have ever assembled."

Coach Hanover smiled and said, "Tell that to the boys who played for me in 1972, and I would bet some of them would want to fight ya." He paused and looked at Shah before saying, "Girl, you must have eye problems, cause someone as pretty as you should never been seen with a joker this ugly."

Shah replied with a touch of sarcasm, "You're not ugly, Coach Hanover."

Coach Hanover pointed at me before saying, "I know, but look at that joker standin' next to you."

We talked about all the events that occurred with the team as well as the big news about Coach Geiger. Coach Hanover said, "I sure hate what has happened to that young man. I hope they fry the hell out of whoever snatched him up."

Before we departed, Coach Hanover asked Shah if he could have a private conversation with me. Before Shah obliged his request, she gave Coach Hanover a kiss goodbye and walked out the room. Coach Hanover smiled when she left the room and said, "You're a lucky man. I think you have a winner in her."

"Yes, sir."

I was about to thank my boss for his support when Coach Hanover spoke up and said, "Before you go, I wanted to thank you. A little bird told me I wouldn't be here..."

I interrupted him and said, "You would have done the same for me."

Coach Hanover raised his hand and said, “Promise me you will do three things for me.”

“What is that, sir?”

“Make sure you let the boys know I miss ‘em, keep makin’ them do the Sidewinder, and for God’s sake, do your very best to protect Frankie Lake from all the buzzards that will be headin’ his way.”

Chapter Eleven

While the investigation into the whereabouts of Coach Geiger continued to dominate the news of Coosawhatchie, the first football game of the season was played against Nixville High School. The entire community rallied around the team and its new interim head coach with one of the largest crowds ever remembered for an opening game. I was so nervous I puked my guts out in the locker room before we took the field. Frankie Lake laughed at me and said, "Mama says spittin' up every now and then is good for the soul."

All along the home sidelines, college head football coaches from around the nation jockeyed for the best possible position not only to see the game, but to be seen by Frankie Lake. Coach Dooley from the University of Georgia was so close to Frankie during one offensive drive, he almost called a play in the first quarter during a crucial third down. Coach Morrison of the University of South Carolina and Coach Ford of Clemson University were standing so close to one another some of the people in Coosawhatchie were accusing the two rival coaches of trying to put a gambling fix on their scheduled matchup much later in November. Coach Paterno from Penn State, yelled in the second quarter at the head referee that he could borrow his glasses after an obvious bad call while Coach Bobby Bowden of Florida State offered the water girl from Coosawhatchie twenty dollars if she could bring him a diet coke from the concession stand.

Behind and around all of the important college head coaches, news reporters from everywhere were fighting hard to position themselves along the sideline of a stadium in a remote part of the Lowcountry of South Carolina. They were all hoping they were in position for the best camera angle possible whenever Frankie Lake accomplished another spectacular athletic achievement.

By halftime, Frankie Lake had run the ball up and down the field like he was a man playing against a bunch of preschoolers. The Nixville bunch did their best, but in the end, Frankie Lake solidified his importance in the college recruiting wars. The play-by-play announcer for the Coosawhatchie Football Radio Network commented at the end of the game, "There ain't nothing fake about Frankie Lake as he picks up where he left off last year. The senior racked up an impressive 385 yards rushing on 19 carries. And your final score is the good guys from Coosa 52 - Nixville - zero."

Not a word was ever mentioned about Doug Pye's fifteen bone shattering tackles or Germaine Mazyck's two interceptions and fumble recovery. Intentionally or not, the local media centered their reporting around Frankie Lake.

That first win started a psychological roll which allowed our team to rattle off four more victories without much effort. People from all over the Lowcountry of South Carolina wanted to witness the team which looked unstoppable. I did my best not to deviate from an offensive plan which was boring but effective. During the second game of the season, when I called the first pass of the year, the fans in the stands let me have it with their vocal displeasure. One man yelled out, "Coach B.B. would never do that."

Although I could sense that not everyone in town was pleased about me being the interim head coach, it was Coach Hanover who called me on a daily basis to give me advice and offer his support. Our relationship changed as I began to think of myself as Coach Hanover's professional equal. Coach Hanover seemed calmer and more relaxed. He never said it, but I sensed that my boss was beginning to really trust me.

During game five of the season, Coach Hanover made an unexpected appearance at a home non-region game against South

Central Savannah. Against doctor's orders, he made his wife take him during the second quarter. He didn't want to make a fuss, but when he entered the stadium the PA announcer spotted him and yelled out, "And let's give a big round of applause to Coach Hanover who has just entered the stadium."

In all of the years he had been coaching at the school, this was Coach Hanover's first standing ovation from the people of Coosawhatchie. Although he appreciated the kindness shown his way, he hated that he was taking attention away from the team.

Two plays later when we fumbled and turned over the ball for the first time of the year, Paige Hanover had to restrain her feisty husband from walking down to the sideline. Four plays later when another of our players muffed a punt giving the ball back to South Central Savannah, Coach Hanover began shouting with a harsh wicked tongue. He used some Korean vocabulary he had not used since he was fighting in a series of battles in the Korean War called Old Baldy. It was all Mrs. Hanover could do to stop him from walking onto the field. As time ran out and halftime began, many of the players walked past Coach Hanover and either gave him a thumbs up, a quick handshake, or a hug. The veteran of many battles became emotional, holding back tears, and not saying a word. He desperately wanted to talk to me about halftime adjustments, but he was physically and emotionally worn out.

Coach Hanover left early that evening while his former players listened to a battle plan in the locker room I was delivering. Two quarters later when the final score indicated that we had destroyed Savannah South Central by a score of 44-7, the perception by many was that Coach Hanover's presence had sparked the team after a sluggish start. The headlines of the *Lowcountry Times* reflected the attitude of an entire community when it read: Hanover's Return Sparks Big Win.

Much later that evening, as Shah and I watched the highlights of the game at my house, a sports reporter from a news channel out of Charleston announced, "When the team ran by Coach Hanover at halftime, he willed them to win the game."

I looked at Shah and said, "Now that's some creative journalism. I guess Coach Hanover was the one at halftime, who changed our defensive front or moved our starting strong safety up on the line of scrimmage."

Shah laughed at me before saying, "I have no idea about what you just said, but I'm smart enough to know that you're not happy about what that reporter said about Coach Hanover."

"I get it that Hanover built this team and this program, but it would be nice if somebody acknowledged that I have kept this thing going. We are undefeated, and the reporters act like I have had nothing to do with it."

"Do I sense an ounce of jealousy in your soul?"

I slumped over on her shoulder while we laid on the couch before replying, "I don't know. Sometimes it's hard to be the one doing all the work and never receiving any attention or credit for what you have done."

Shah, with a serious look on her face raised her voice saying, "Tell me about it. My student's math scores continue to rise, but believe me- nobody cares. Guess what, I do it for the kids; not for some pat on the back from people who have no idea what I do to prepare my kids for success. You better get off your high horse. Right this minute, Mister."

I didn't want to admit that she was right, and for a moment I said nothing. I then gave her a big hug. "You're right. I'm sorry for that pity party."

Shah then asked me, "I think you need to ask yourself why you love coaching. Are you doing it for the glory of the wins and losses or are you doing it so that you can have a positive impact on the young men that you meet along the journey?"

I nodded yes, but in my heart, I wasn't sure. I then thought about the sacrifices she had made for her students. A few moments later she said, "The winning is nice, but your impact on the young lives you encounter will be what is most important."

After I listened to what she had to say, I made up my mind that I would try to be a better coach. I was also convinced that Shah was the person I wanted to marry. For the first time in our relationship, I recognized how her deep insight along with her giving heart were indeed everything I had ever wanted in a life partner.

* * *

While we were talking about how I needed to get my professional priorities in order, two redneck brothers drove down a remote dirt road fifty miles away near a small town across the Georgia state line called Egypt. The two brothers didn't say a word to each other as they drove slowly down the long dirt road through a swampy area about three miles from the Turkey Branch Baptist Church. After parking their truck under an enormous willow tree which was tangled with years of wild kudzu and Spanish moss, they hopped out of a company truck, took off a small cooler and two plastic jugs of water from the bed of the truck. They carried all of the items deeper in the swamp.

Ten minutes later they came to a well- hidden hunting lodge protected by a large metal gate and enough barbed wire to keep the most adventurous animal or person away. Once inside the building after unlocking two chained locks, they found Coach Jaden Geiger laying on an old mattress dead asleep. The light of a small lamp in the corner of the room indicated that he had eaten his lunch. When they woke him to give him fresh water, a home cooked meal with meatloaf, mashed potatoes, and vegetables along with a fresh bar of soap, Coach Geiger shouted at the masked brothers, "I swear if you let me go, I won't tell anyone about this." He kept rambling.

The two brothers remained silent as the largest one held a pistol in his hand. They gave Coach Geiger a fresh set of clothes, and led him to a rustic bathroom. Dragging a long cable wire attached to a long metal pole in the bedroom, Coach Geiger was able to shower and take care of his personal hygiene business. After he changed into his fresh clothes one of the brothers looked at Coach Geiger and said, "Be patient. We've told you over and over that you will be here for a while... Nobody wants to hurt you. Later this week we'll let you go outside for a few hours if you can behave. We'll see you again in the morning."

The brothers took off their masks once they hopped into their pickup truck. The older, Jimmy, looked at his Jerry and said, "The boss says we have to keep him a few more months."

Jerry nodded his head and said, "All of this would have been a lot easier if we had just killed him."

"The boss said it's important that he is not harmed. When the time is right, we'll let him off on the Interstate at the state line fatter and healthier lookin' than the night we picked him up."

Jerry said, "Ok, but this week you're gonna wash his laundry, and I'll do the cookin'."

"Deal."

* * *

The next Sunday afternoon before I headed to the school to break down film, I decided to stop and visit with Coach Hanover and pick his mind. I had been to his small brick ranch style house several times over the past two years. This day was different. When I entered the carport, Coach Hanover had already opened the screen door of the kitchen entrance before I had a chance to knock. As I walked through the kitchen, I could feel the warmth of a house heated with a gas stove. The warmth of the gas heat on a cool October day felt different from the electric heat at my place. It wasn't just the heat that made me feel different on this day. I was nervous because I truly wanted his advice about my relationship with Shah. I didn't know how to broach the subject. I wasn't even sure if he would care. For whatever reason I wanted to know what he thought.

I picked my fingernails as I listened to him talk about the next upcoming opponent as if he were coaching the team. He then offered me a glass of sweet ice tea.

I nodded before saying, “Yes, sir.”

While he poured the tea, he smiled and said, “You evidently did a hell of a job with the defense after I left the game.”

I thanked him for his words of praise and then said, “I did the exact same thing you would have done. I learned it all from the master of defense.”

Coach Hanover replied, “You’re a much better coach than me. It took me two years to figure out what I was doing. Hell, you already know ten times more about being a head football coach than I ever dreamed about.”

I took his compliments with gratitude; however, I quickly changed the subject when I said, “I need to ask you your advice on a personal matter.”

Before I could say what was on my mind, Paige Hanover walked into the kitchen and gave me a big hug. She then poured herself a glass of sweet tea and said, “Lord knows I almost had to tackle this one from going onto the field Friday night. I’m thankful that you will be playing on the road this week. I don’t think I could rope him in two weeks in a row.”

I nodded my head and said nothing. Coach Hanover then looked at me and asked, “So what advice do you need from me?”

I momentarily hesitated while glancing at Paige. Coach Hanover quickly said, “Whatever you have to say, you can say in front of my sweetheart.”

I said, louder than I’d intended, “I’m going to ask Shah to marry me.”

I sat at the kitchen table for several seconds waiting for their reaction. Paige smiled and said, “Congratulations, but Stephen, you better make sure that she can handle being a coach's wife. Being a coach's wife is more than getting use to the long hours; it's being able to hold back with your tongue during the times when some jerk in the bleachers screams at your husband; it's being able to handle unexpected gossip you hear about your husband; it's being able to continue to go to church when you know good and well that a few people are praying for your husband to fail."

Coach Hanover added, "I know you love her, but Paige is right. Make sure Shah understands before she commits to somethin' that she may later regret. Congratulations. I think she is an outstandin' young lady."

I thanked both of them before saying that I expected them to come to the wedding if Shah accepted my proposal.

Paige asked, "When do you intend to ask her and where?"

"I'm not sure. I was thinking that I would drive her down to Charleston one weekend afternoon and ask her at the same spot we first kissed."

Coach Hanover asked, "Where was that?"

"On a stretch of the Battery in front of Rainbow Row."

Paige laughed and said, "I'm glad this old fool didn't ask me at the place we first kissed."

"Oh, where was that?"

"Our first kiss was on the seat of a Ferguson tractor in the middle of a fifty-acre corn field. He was showing me how to plow a field. If he had asked me to marry him on that tractor, it would have never happened. Take Shah to a nice place to eat in Charleston and pop the question to her in some fancy restaurant."

Chapter Twelve

The recruiting wars intensified over the next few weeks as college coaches began asking me which colleges were still in the hunt and which colleges didn't stand a chance. Even if I knew the answers, I would not have revealed what I knew. The truth of the matter was that I knew nothing. Whenever I talked to Frankie about which schools interested him the most, he would either smile, stare off into space, or say, "I likes them all."

Each time I pressed Frankie to narrow down his list of potential schools, Frankie would decline. Finally, during the week of the ninth game of the season, I made Frankie do what Frankie had been avoiding. I made Frankie write down his top ten schools on a piece of yellow legal pad paper.

Later that afternoon, I gave a phone call to local sports reporter, Gerald Davis at the *Lowcountry Times*. "Hey, Gerald, you can thank me later, but I wanted you to be the first person to know Frankie Lake's top ten list of schools he is considering."

When I read out the names of the colleges, Gerald laughed uncontrollably when I read the name of the last school on the list. Gerald then snorted back through his laughter, "Give me a break. Does he even know where the University of Wyoming is located?"

I laughed with him before replying, "I have no idea."

Gerald asked, "Do you mind if I come down before practice and do an interview with Frankie to coincide with what you told me?"

"Sure. You better hurry because we start practice in about an hour."

After I hung up the phone, I heard a knock at the office door.

I yelled, "Come in."

Standing at the door, one of my senior football players said, "Coach, Mrs. Shrader in the front office sent me down here to give you your mail and messages."

Shuffling through the mail and several messages, one stood out. It read, "Call Coach Ford at Clemson ASAP."

I wasted no time contacting Coach Ford. I felt lucky when he picked up on the first ring.

"Hey, Coach, this is Coach Blake at Coosawhatchie, I'm returning your call."

Like old friends, we chatted about both of our football seasons before Coach Ford complimented me by saying, "I wish my defense was playing as good as yours right now. We are still strugglin' a bit, but thank the Lord we have turned the season around after a painfully slow start."

After we talked a few minutes more, Ford finally asked, "So where do we stand with Frankie?"

I replied with a confident voice, "You guys are at the top of his list."

"That's great news. I would like to go ahead and arrange for him to come to a game this weekend. We play NC State, and I think it will be a good atmosphere for him to experience."

"I'll certainly ask him if he wants to go to the game and I'll let you know."

While I was still talking to Coach Ford, Gerald Davis of the *Lowcountry Times* walked right into the coach's office. I thanked Coach Ford and hung up the phone.

Gerald smiled and said, "I see Danny is doing his best to sign Frankie."

I slid back in my chair and replied, "These guys are relentless. Coach Morrison, Coach Bowden, Coach Majors, and Coach Dye both called earlier. All of them are dying for Frankie to come and visit. The truth is that Frankie does not want to visit. Whenever I bring up that he needs to go visit some of these places, he always says that wherever he decides to attend college, he will have four years to see all he will need to see."

"He does have a point." Gerald then smiled big before he continued, "Maybe Frankie knows that things tend to change once the college coaches lure the recruits on campus far away from everyone else. I've seen kids go on a visit to a college campus and come back with a whole different attitude."

"Why is that?"

"I don't know, but I think it has something to do with each school's nightlife, all the beer and liquor that's available. Don't forget about the wild women, the wild women they use to seduce those kids. You know that some schools have better looking women than others. I wish I was seventeen again and being recruited by some Division One school. I might get in trouble."

I quickly said, "Frankie is not like that. If they try those shenanigans with him it will backfire."

Gerald laughed and said, "You better wake up, Coach. He's a teenager and these sharks know exactly how to push the right buttons. One sweet thing dressed the way they dress these days, and Lord have mercy, there is no telling what a young man will do. Don't forget all of the backhanded promises that take place that we know nothing about. I have to believe it's a slimy business. Some of those recruits who visit for a weekend receive an education long before they become students."

I stood up, walked over to the office door and closed it. I then looked at Gerald and said, "I really do worry about Frankie. What I'm telling you is confidential. Can I trust that I won't read about this in tomorrow's paper?"

Gerald put up his hand and said, "Scout's honor. Whenever Coach Hanover and I talked in private we have always had a long-standing agreement that the stories from Korea he shared with me would never be printed in the paper. Neither would the back stories that came from practices, games, or the locker room. I have never published anything without his consent. Same goes for you, now."

I thanked him and then whispered, "I don't know how in the world Frankie will be able to keep up academically at any college he attends. I'm afraid that his SAT scores are bogus."

"Why do you say that?"

"Frankie is not dumb, but he is academically challenged. I believe he has a learning disability, but his parents will not allow him to be tested. They have never wanted him to take Special Education classes. He really struggles. Coach Hanover and I worry about him because we have tutored him. Just between you and me, when I saw his test scores, I could not believe his scores were higher than some of our honor students. At first, I didn't say anything about it, but then I did some checking. On the day that he took the test, a teacher here at school who was scheduled to administer the test called in sick. No big deal. Well, it turns out it was a big deal. Then the person who did show up to administer the test supposedly came from Savannah. To this day, nobody seems to know who that person was. When the school tried to send him his paycheck, the postal service sent the check back. They informed the front office that the address didn't exist. I checked the phone directory in Savannah and guess what? There is no Mr. Timmy Zeller listed."

Gerald said, 'What you're telling me does sound strange but that doesn't prove the test was altered."

"Frankie told me the truth."

"What truth?"

"He said that when he turned in his answer sheet that afternoon, he saw Mr. Zeller place his answer sheet into his briefcase which was sitting on top of the desk. Frankie didn't think too much of it, but he noticed that Mr. Zeller didn't place the other student's answer sheets inside of his briefcase. He told me that he clearly saw Mr. Zeller pull out another answer sheet from a folder and place it with the other student's answer sheets before he walked up to the guidance office and turned them in." I paused and then continued, "I feel confident that Frankie's original answer sheet was never graded. On top of all that, the teacher here at our school who called in sick, no longer works in this district. She is an assistant principal at a nice school in Charleston, and she refused to speak to me."

Gerald tried to be funny saying, "Don't lose any sleep over that. I bet it was the University of Wyoming who financed that stunt."

"I know I shouldn't care, but I do. It really burns me up. I'm afraid that Frankie is going to fail if he ever has to do any real college academic work."

"I wouldn't worry too much about that. These days, every school has tutors that do the most of the work for the athletes. Lord knows some of the ones I have interviewed in the past twenty years weren't ever accused of being the next Albert Einstein. It's a sad situation, but nobody cares as long as those athletes can run, jump, tackle, and score. College football is becoming big business and it will only get bigger. One day, in the near future, these college football coaches will make big bucks. The television revenue is unbelievable. You mark my words. One day college head football coaches will make more than a quarter of a million dollars a year."

I laughed before saying, "That will never happen. Nobody is worth that kind of money."

A few minutes later, Frankie entered the coach's office before practice. I sat beside him in a metal folding chair as Gerald Davis began an exclusive interview for the *Lowcountry Times*. They talked about the season and the next upcoming game for a few minutes before Gerald turned on a tape recorder. He then asked Frankie how he had narrowed down his list of possible schools he would attend the next year. Frankie seemed confused, finally saying, "I likes all of them."

Gerald rephrased the question by asking, "How did you pick the top ten schools?"

"All the schools are nice."

Gerald looked at me and raised his eyebrows before he asked, "Would you say that any of the schools is your favorite right now?"

"Yes, sir, I likes all of them."

I corrected Frankie and said, "You like all of them."

Frankie smiled and said, "I forgot. I like all of them."

Gerald moved on by asking, "What do you want to do when you graduate from college?"

"Go to works."

Gerald scratched his head before saying, "Yes, I understand, but what kind of work would you like to do?"

"I like drivin' my Daddy's truck, and I like animals."

Gerald asked, "So you would like to be a mechanical engineer or a veterinarian?

"No, sir, I'd like to drive a truck or raise some pigs."

I couldn't help but smile. I then said, "Frankie, that was good. It's about time for practice. You go ahead and get ready."

"Thanks, Coach."

I then yelled at him as he began walking out of the office, "Hey, I almost forgot. Coach Ford called a few minutes ago. Clemson wants you to come to their football game this weekend. They play NC State. It would be a great opportunity for you to see the campus."

Frankie stopped in the hallway before saying, "Wish I could, but I have to helps my Pops on Saturday. Mama always cuts my hair on Saturday afternoons so I don't know when I'll be able to goes. Please tell them I said thank you."

After Frankie left the office, I looked at Gerald and said, "See what I mean? The boy does not want to leave his home. It's amazing." I then glared at Gerald. "If you print any of that interview, I'll kill you."

"Coach, I'm way ahead of you." He then pushed the rewind button on the tape recorder and began erasing the tape. "All I'll do is publish Frankie's top ten picks. That news alone will have the colleges going crazy. Especially for the alumni and boosters at the University of Wyoming. Now that I think of it, I'm not sure I know where Wyoming is located. God help us."

Chapter Thirteen

The next week, Frankie's Top Ten list made national news. However, it didn't dissuade those colleges, who didn't make the list from sending more mail and assistant football coaches to the small town of Coosawhatchie. I had assumed that the list would discourage many of them, but it didn't. It seemed to have the opposite effect as many colleges and universities increased their presence. Coach Treadway from Virginia Tech tried to persuade me to allow only the top ten schools to be on campus. When I ran that idea by Coach Hanover with a quick telephone call, Hanover told me that it would hurt the other boys chances to be seen by other schools. He rejected the idea.

New coaches with new sales tactics showed up from all over the nation. When the University of Wyoming Head Football Coach Al Kincaid showed up unannounced, I wanted to tell him that he was wasting his time, but I kept quiet. Coach Kincaid informed me that the entire state of Wyoming was ecstatic about making Frankie's Top Ten List.

* * *

Fifty miles away in a swamp not far from the small town of Egypt, Georgia, Coach Jaden Geiger's days of being cooped up in a remote hunting lodge ended when the masked brothers Jimmy and Jerry took him on a short walk around the property. News concerning his abduction had died down in the media along with the candle light vigils and law enforcement press conferences. It was as if Coach Geiger was a forgotten man.

That morning, as he walked, followed by the masked brothers at gunpoint, he asked, "So can you at least tell me why I'm being held?"

Jerry, the dumber of the pair, said, "We ain't supposed to talk to you. Our boss told us to keep our mouths shut."

"Your boss must be a pretty important man around here."

"Most of his business is across the state line..."

Jimmy punched his younger brother in the ribs. "Shut the hell up."

A few minutes later after they had walked next to the swamp and turned back around toward the hunting lodge, Geiger asked, "Can you at least tell me the date of today? I lost count a few days ago."

Jerry muttered, "It's the first week of November."

Coach Geiger pressed harder by asking, "Can you tell me any news from around the world?"

Jerry said, "Clemson done beat NC State..."

Jimmy cried out, "Jerry, I told you... Crap..." Jimmy then realized he had inadvertently revealed the name of his brother. He quickly looked at Coach Geiger and said, "You didn't hear that."

"Heard what?"

"Jimmy, you just told him my name."

"No crap, you idiot. Now he knows both of our names."

* * *

Saturday afternoon Shah could tell that I was nervous when we headed for Charleston. While I was driving, I kept putting my hand in my right pants pocket to make sure I still had the diamond engagement ring I had bought a few days prior. Coach Hanover sent me to one of his former players who owned a pawn shop in Savannah. His former player told me the ring came from an estate sale. He also told me that since I worked for Coach Hanover, he would let me have the ring for his cost.

As Shah kept talking, I could only think about what I was going to say to her when I asked her the most important question of my life. I kept driving.

Shah suddenly screamed, "What are you doing?"

"What do you mean?"

"It looks like you're digging for gold. Do you have jock itch?"

"Yeah, something like that."

Forty-five minutes later we were being seated at the Poogan's Porch Restaurant on Queen Street in Charleston. My parents had splurged and brought our entire family to the same restaurant when I graduated from the Citadel. I loved the food and I knew it would be the right atmosphere for an engagement.

Shah couldn't believe I had brought her to one of Charleston's most elegant places to dine once she looked at the prices on the menu. I never told her, but I had to dip into my savings.

She said, "How can you afford this?"

"The price is irrelevant. I want you to order whatever makes you happy."

"Ok, but I still can't believe you're not breaking down film like you do on most weekend afternoons."

"I needed a break. Football can wait for a few hours."

She never knew that I would be staying up all night breaking down film after we headed back to Coosawhatchie. I wanted everything that night to be perfect, but deep down I also wanted it to be over so that I could get back to the business of game preparation.

She asked, "Have you ever eaten She Crab soup?"

I don't really remember what we ate that night after her bowl of She Crab soup was delivered to our table. I slowly pulled the diamond ring out of my pocket. I dropped it under the table. I quickly reached down, then quickly stood up from my chair, and knelt down on one knee in front of the entire restaurant. I then asked her to be my bride. A standing ovation by the patrons of Poogan's Porch Restaurant signaled that she had accepted my proposal. Through a few tears and hugs we did our best to eat our meals before we drove to my parent's home on James Island to start spreading the news.

That night, after my parents insisted that we call Shah's parents to give them the news, I looked over at my father and knew that he was happy. He was a tough military man, who seldom showed his emotions, but when my mother patted him on the back, I saw a few tears rolling down his cheeks. He said, "I know you have to go back to Coosawhatchie tonight, but when football season is over, we would love to throw a large engagement party in your honor. You did good, son."

* * *

The cold November winds blowing off the coast of South Carolina brought with them high expectations for a state championship season in Coosawhatchie as our team finished the regular season undefeated heading into the playoffs. November also was the month that his doctors told Coach Hanover that he could not return to work until January. The old veteran of the Korean War didn't like what he heard and vocally protested with his cardiologist until the cardiologist finally told him it was a matter of life and death.

When I heard the news, I called Coach Hanover and told him that I would try my best to have the team prepared to win a championship. After our phone conversation, I could tell that Coach Hanover was fighting depression. I tried to cheer him up but it was no use.

We ended up blowing out the competition during the first two playoff games. Everyone in town knew that the third-round playoff matchup might be the stiffest competition that we would face.

While the students at Coosawhatchie County High School were all preparing for the Thanksgiving Holiday, I was very concerned about Appleton High School, which had some of the biggest lineman in the state. Coach Hanover told me, "That offensive line from Appleton looks like a bunch of semi-trucks rollin' down the interstate. You might have to go under 'em, over 'em, and around 'em to beat this bunch."

On the Tuesday before the big game, I called Frankie into my office to discuss his official visits to the colleges that he was most interested in. I explained to Frankie that he needed to take some official visits and that he could decide which head coaches could come and visit with him and his family in January. I then pulled out a calendar and said, "We need to go ahead and make a plan so you and your folks can decide which college you would like to attend."

Frankie smiled and gave the same answer he had been giving all along. He grinned and said in correct English, "I like them all."

I was trying hard to be patient but my patience was wearing thin. With the pressure of the big game, and wedding plans, I snapped when I yelled at the most innocent soul I had ever encountered, "You listen to me, Frankie, time is running out. You have to make a decision." I instantly regretted it.

Frankie didn't flinch. "Ok. I trust you coach. Whichever ones you say, will be good enough for me."

Those words shook my soul because now, I would be the one to decide which colleges were in the hunt. With one quick reply from Frankie, I was now in charge of the future for the nation's most highly recruited football player.

Once Frankie left the office, I pulled out and looked at Frankie's Top Ten List. I began to feel nauseous. Unlike anything I had ever experienced as a coach, I felt an enormous amount of self-inflicted pressure to make the right decision for a young man that had inadvertently impacted my life in a positive way. I thought about Frankie's innocence and hated that Frankie was being thrown into the recruiting wars of college football. It bothered me that Frankie would soon be subjected to some of the ugliness of the real world. I then thought about the relationships I had made with some of the nation's finest recruiters. I, like Frankie, liked them all. I then realized that I was the adult in this situation, and

Frankie, of all people, needed my protection, guidance, and wisdom concerning this matter.

Late that afternoon, long after practice had concluded, I heard a knock on the outside door of the gym. Looking down the hallway of the gym, I could see Coach Treadway of Virginia Tech knocking on the door. When I opened the door, Treadway said, "Follow me to Henry's Barbecue. I'm starving, and I owe you dinner."

I shook my head back and forth saying, "I don't..."

Coach Treadway grabbed my arm and begged, "I need you. I can't eat by myself. All my other coaching buddies are on the road somewhere else tonight. The least you can do is keep me from having to eat by myself."

* * *

For the next thirty minutes, I listened to the most entertaining college recruiter I had met. While we ate our dinner, I listened to the animated coach of defense explain how he had an interesting time in Virginia Beach the week before while conducting an official home visit with a big-time recruit. The recruit's father insisted that Coach Treadway strip down in his boxers and drink a few adult beverages with him and the recruit's step mother while they relaxed in a hot tub on the back deck of their trailer. Coach Treadway was able to land the young man because he gained the father's trust.

In between bites of food and customers stopping by our table to wish me good luck regarding the upcoming playoff game, Coach Treadway told more tales about his recruiting adventures. After our waitress refilled our drinks, I changed the subject by opening up to Coach Treadway. I confided to him the dilemma concerning Frankie's recruitment. I didn't plan to spill the beans, but I trusted Coach Treadway. "I don't know what to do. Frankie doesn't want to visit any of these colleges. He does not want to leave home."

"You know I want to sign him like everyone else, but if I were you, I would forget it. If he does not want to go on any visits, so be it."

"But don't you think he needs to actually visit some of these places before he makes a decision? I feel confident that Frankie has no earthly idea where any of these colleges are located."

"Who cares? I've had kids sign with me whose only knowledge of our place was from a fancy brochure. You need to let this go. Once Frankie makes a final decision, the rest will be history."

Out of nowhere, interrupting our conversation, Henry Bozzard plopped himself down next to Coach Treadway and said, "Well, if this ain't a nice little reunion between you two."

I then reintroduced Coach Treadway to Henry. Treadway said, "You sure do have some of the best barbeque I have ever tasted."

Henry glared at him and replied, "You have that wrong, my friend. This has been voted as the best barbeque in the world. Look over there at the sign hangin' on the wall."

Coach Treadway quickly asked, "Now did you paint that sign yourself or did you have someone paint it for you? That's a pretty clever gimmick."

Offended by that question, Henry stood up and said, "Please excuse us, Coach, I need to have a quick conversation with Coach Blake in my office concerning the team's pregame meal this week." He then turned and walked to the back of the restaurant.

I looked at Coach Treadway, put up my hands and said, "I'll be back in a few minutes."

Once inside Henry's huge office, I was surprised when Henry shut the door and shouted, "What in the hell do you think you're doin' comin' in here eatin' with that smart ass from Virginia?"

"Who do you think you're talking to, Henry. I'll eat with whoever I want to eat with."

Sensing he had been too abrasive, Henry changed his tone saying, "You don't get it. He's the enemy."

"Whose enemy?"

"Our enemy."

"What in the hell are you talking about?"

"The only thing that smart ass wants is for Frankie to sign with Virginia Tech. We can't let that happen."

"We who?"

Henry growled back at me, "Me and you. We have a civic obligation to do everything we can to make sure that Henry does not leave our great state. He needs to sign with the most trusted coach in college football, Coach Danny Ford."

"Why not with Coach Morrison at South Carolina?"

"Look, Coach, I like Joe Morrison, but Frankie does not need to be cramped up in that city school. What matters most is that Frankie needs the wide-open spaces of Clemson University. That would be the best thing for him."

I did my best to keep my voice down when I replied, "Frankie and his family will decide what is best for them."

Henry growled again. "You don't really believe that. A kid like Frankie needs—"

"I've heard enough. This conversation is over."

* * *

My conversation with Coach Treadway was cut short that evening; however, my conversation with Shah heated up when I arrived home and called her on the phone. She lit into me like she had never done before. She was agitated that I had decided to eat out without calling her and letting her know that I would be late. I tried to smooth it over, realizing that she had experienced a tough day at work. She wouldn't stop. In a few short minutes a shouting match over the phone ensued. We were having our first real fight as a couple and it was on the phone.

She told me that she was tired of me being inconsiderate. I told her that I was tired of her constant nagging about things that were not important. We argued about our Thanksgiving Day plans since

I would be practicing with the team early on Thanksgiving morning. Then out of nowhere, she broached the subject that we had both been avoiding. Shah screamed, "I want you to know that if we ever have children, they will be raised Muslim."

Those words hit me like a shattered bottle cutting into my soul. I didn't respond immediately. Her words were not expected nor was the emotional pain I felt when she voiced them. Eventually I recovered enough to yell back, "Our children will be baptized in the Catholic church like their father. He or she will be raised Christian."

Back and forth, we wrestled over a topic that neither one of us seemed to care about when we fell in love. Now, we both deeply cared about how our future children would be educated regarding the spiritual world. Neither of us were experts on the theology concerning our own religion, but when Shah talked about the only God of the universe being Allah, I simply said, "I have been raised to believe that a person's belief in Jesus is the only way to eternal life."

This debate lasted longer than expected as both of us began sharing scriptures from the Bible and the Quran; something we had never done. I relied on what I had learned as a child about my faith. I began to wander down my own path of religious awareness as I stated my beliefs for the first time in my life. Shah listened and tried to counter my explanations with her limited knowledge about her own religion. As we both continued to search for ways in which the two religions were similar, it was Shah who said, "The way I see it we both believe in one God and that one God is the judge of us when we meet him at our death. I'm willing to concede that it's not that simple; however, I have no problem with our children being baptized in the Catholic Church."

I was stunned. I didn't expect her radical change of heart. She then said, "Don't act like I'm crazy. My parents' best friends are Jewish. It's not like I was raised going to the Mosque every week.

The only thing I ask is that you allow me to teach our children about some of my family's Islamic traditions concerning food and holidays."

I smiled before replying, "You never cease to amaze me. I love you, Shah, and God loves you, too."

She laughed and abruptly changed the subject. "You know that we don't need to spend a lot money for a big wedding. We could have a simple ceremony here or in Charleston. Why don't we go ahead and make plans to have our wedding during our Christmas vacation?"

"You don't want to get married in New Jersey?"

"Not a chance. I didn't have many girl friends back home so it will not bother me in the least to have the wedding here. My parents would love to come to Charleston anyway."

Chapter Fourteen

The next morning at Coosawhatchie County High School was a half day for the Thanksgiving Break. Outside of my classroom, I threw two Tylenol down my throat, chased by my first taste of the "New Coke" that was being promoted all over the nation. I looked at Coach Fulmer from the University of Tennessee, who was standing next to the doorway of my classroom and said, "This stuff is absolutely terrible. Why in the world would the Coca Cola Corporation decide to change the formula of the most popular product in the history of soft drinks?"

Fulmer laughed out loud. "Some people couldn't be happy if they worked in a cake factory." He paused for a few seconds and said, "It looks like you had a late night of partying."

I raised my eyebrows and dropped my briefcase in the hallway next to my classroom. "You have no idea." I then pulled out a wad of school keys and unlocked my classroom door.

Coach Fulmer picked up my briefcase and handed it to me while saying, "Big game this Friday. I wanted to wish you the best before you become too busy this morning. I'll be flying back to Knoxville in a few hours. Whenever your season ends, we would love to have Frankie come and visit with us in Knoxville one weekend."

"Coach, I'll do everything I can to make that happen, but as of right now, Frankie does not want to visit anyone. I think he is scared to leave home."

Fulmer patted me on my back before saying, "Don't worry about it. You can't make him go. If it makes you feel any better, I run across this all the time, especially with kids who have never flown before. By the time January rolls around most of them who are hesitant to take a flight, change their minds. I have a feeling that Frankie will do the same. It's funny how peer pressure affects these kids when friends and family begin asking them about which colleges they are going to visit."

"I hate to tell you this, but Frankie is not like everyone else. He could care less what everybody thinks. He is the most innocent soul I have ever met."

* * *

Thursday morning's practice was special for our team, our coaches, and an entire community. It had been four long years since Coosawhatchie County High School had made it this far in the playoffs and enjoyed the civic celebration of a Thanksgiving morning practice. Something that was once a Coosawhatchie tradition had now returned. Coach Hanover always made the Thanksgiving morning practices special. I knew nothing about the Coosawhatchie volunteer fire department bringing out the fire truck and parking it next to the practice field with red lights flashing. I had never witnessed the booster club members bringing ham biscuits, slices of pound cake, and small Dixie cups filled with orange juice for the boys and coaches. No one bothered to tell me that three local pastors would say a few words to the team, offering prayers of strength and safety. It all was just as new as the joy of running out onto the practice field with a hundred or so men, women, and children hollering, "Coosa, Coosa, Coosa." To top it off, many people in the community had dropped off bags filled with candy and homemade cards of well wishes for each player and coach. All this was put in place by Coach Hanover many years ago during his first state championship season, and now it continued anew.

* * *

By the time the bus load of Appleton High School giants rolled into the city limits of Coosawhatchie the next day, most of the home side of the stadium was already packed with fans. I could not believe how many people were already inside of the stadium when two of my assistant coaches and myself put out the sideline markers and end zone pylons a few hours before kickoff. When I saw an ESPN truck and several regional news station vans parked near the stadium, I felt nervous. After watching the visiting team walk to their locker room, I couldn't remember ever seeing a team with such large linemen. They looked bigger than some of the teams I played on at the Citadel.

During my pregame speech that evening, I jumped up on a table in the locker room and cried out, "I know some of you don't believe me, but this is going to be a battle. These guys are big and strong. Have no regrets when this is over."

Once again, in addition to the fans, the stadium was packed with college football coaches from around the nation. I noticed that all of the college head football coaches from Frankie's top ten list were in attendance. I had heard earlier that the Savannah airport had never witnessed such an impressive fleet of Lear jets.

On the first play from scrimmage, I called for a play-action pass to start out the game. Appleton's defense, thinking that Frankie Lake would run the ball, was caught off guard when our receiver flew by the defense and was wide open. Scoring so easily, some of our players were laughing when they came off the field after the extra point. I yelled at them, "Stop that crap. This is going to be a tough game; the toughest you've ever played."

On the sidelines that night, rivals Coach Morrison and Coach Ford stayed away from each other so that the news media wouldn't talk about them like they had done before. Coach Dooley from Georgia and his brother Bill from Virginia Tech also didn't speak until they left the stadium. Coach Paterno and Coach Schembechler joked about how some of the people in the crowd were acting like they were freezing when the temperature was only 42 degrees. Coach Bobby Bowden was dressed in a Florida State coat which resembled a parka while Coach Majors of Tennessee and Coach Dye of Auburn both wore short sleeve white shirts and a tie. Coach Kincaid from the University of Wyoming had them all beat as he wore a ten-gallon cowboy hat adorned with an eagle feather, long black cowboy boots, a brown thick shirt, and a Wyoming bolo tie. Some of the people in the stands thought he was the mascot.

After that surprise opening score, the game changed drastically. Back and forth both teams went up and down the field in the first half but neither team scored a point. When the second quarter was over, we were holding on to a slim 7-0 lead. For the first time since I was named the interim head football coach, I verbally jumped all over Frankie for not running hard enough while I blasted the offensive line for committing three holding penalties. I was rough on them for a few minutes until one of my assistant coaches whispered to me that Coach Hanover had sent a message wanting me to know how proud he was of the defense. Before we left the locker room, I shouted at the team, "Now go out and have fun. Enjoy yourselves because we are about to head to the state championship game."

* * *

The next morning headlines for the *Lowcountry Times* read: Blake Takes Coosa to the Finals. I could not believe the article in the paper which talked about how I had done a good job taking over the program during Coach Hanover's absence. I didn't know it at the time, but a few blocks away, Hanover's daughter read the article and was furious. She called her mother that morning and said, "They act like he is the savior of the football program. Daddy never had an article written about him that nice."

Listening to the telephone exchange in the background, Coach Hanover yelled at his daughter, "He deserves the credit. He has them playing great. Whenever you beat Appleton by five touchdowns, you have done something."

Although the veteran coach was sincere with his comments to his daughter, a part of him was envious of what had been accomplished during his absence. He couldn't wait to get back to coaching and was hurt that he wasn't able to finish out this season. To his credit he never once complained, and he squashed any rumors in the town that he didn't get along with me. Whenever others had said something negative about my coaching, it had been and would continue to be Coach Hanover who supported me more than anyone else in the community.

* * *

That Saturday afternoon, while college football teams around the nation played their games, Shah and I rode around the town of Coosawhatchie looking for any homes that were for sale. While we drove for almost an hour, we made plans for a wedding that would take place sometime after the state championship game in December. After looking for homes with no success, we stopped at the Coosa Food King grocery store to do some shopping. Inside the store we were unexpectedly greeted by several people we didn't know. They wished us luck for the upcoming state championship game. One old white lady yelled, "We love our boys. Get them right, Coach."

An older black gentleman dressed in a nice suit said, "We are with you, Coach. Keep up the good work."

After we completed our shopping and made it to the checkout line, the manager of the store walked over to us and said, "Your money's no good here. Thank you for taking us back to the state championship game."

"What are you talking about?"

The manager said, "Tiger Don came in here the other day and told me that for the month of December, your groceries would be charged to his account. I'm just followin' orders."

* * *

The next week was a whirlwind of activities including pep rallies, prayer services, feasts prepared for the team, college recruiters making last minute pitches, and news media reporters trying their best to get a scoop about a team led by the nation's top prospect. When the town put up a billboard which read: ONE MORE WIN, Frankie and I laughed when we drove by on our way to school Tuesday morning. School was in session for educational purposes, but it was evident to everyone that students, faculty, and administrators were only interested in talking about the big game.

Coach Treadway, Coach Fulmer, Coach Aldridge, and Coach Kenney all brought the front office secretaries at the school several boxes of Danishes, expensive chocolates, and a big bottle of wine to show their appreciation for allowing them to hang out in the front office the entire school year. Principal Dean became the most popular man in the county that morning when he announced over the loudspeaker that there would be no school on Friday so that everyone could head to the state championship game in Columbia at Williams-Brice Stadium.

I was so busy making administrative arrangements for our travel to the state championship game, I had little time to prepare for the quickest team we had faced all year. The Antreville Cougars from the upstate of South Carolina played a style of football that Coach Hanover described to me as "scrappy and salty."

I had asked Hanover to review the game films of Antreville and offer any suggestions. It was a bitter-sweet assignment for Coach Hanover; however, the feisty coaching veteran reviewed the films and found something of great significance. When he met with me to discuss what he had found, I looked at him and said, "Coach, you're a genius. How in the world did you pick that up?"

What Coach Hanover found was an offensive indicator that nobody else had noticed during the entire season. Prudent film break down proved that the fullback for Antreville unknowingly was tipping off the defense as to what kind of play his team was running. Coach Hanover smiled when he showed me that the fullback leaned forward in his stance whenever it was a run. Whenever it was a pass play, the fullback rocked back in his stance. Coach's Hanover's detailed analysis was true one hundred percent of the time. Knowing whether a play was a run or a pass before it occurred would be almost like cheating, but Antreville's flaw was there for any opponent to see. Coach Hanover wrote in detail how the young men from Antreville should be defended with the knowledge he had found through intense film study. I then asked an obvious question, "What if we build our whole game plan around one player's stance and that player has to leave the game for an injury?"

Coach Hanover turned on the projector and said, "Look at the film. I knew you would ask that question. If you look at the fullback in this game, it's a different player. I have looked and evidently the stance problem is something some coach is teachin' his players to do. All of their fullbacks do the same thing. I'm sure if Coach Frost knew this information, he would fire whoever's teachin' this."

I thanked my boss and said, "Coach, I'm sorry that you will not be able to coach this Friday."

"I'll be there, but my doctor says there is no sideline for me. Everything works out for the best."

Chapter Fifteen

A week of celebration and anticipation came to a climax on Friday when an entire community prepared to leave their homes and businesses to make the 125-mile journey to Columbia. When I realized that many of my players had never been to the capital city of their state, I changed their departure time and arranged for us to take a few tours. Shah took it upon herself to help me by making the necessary phone calls, putting together an itinerary, and drawing a map that would show us how to make our way through Columbia to Williams-Brice stadium. Members of the booster club made more sandwiches and snacks for the trip than we needed. Shah told me, "They act like you're going on a cross-country excursion. I can't believe all the food they're preparing. You could stop by Fort Jackson and feed all the troops with what they are planning."

When Henry Bozzard tried to put a banner on the team's rented Trailways bus, I refused when I saw that it read: Lake Express. I scolded Henry by saying, "This is a team effort."

Several local politicians and pastors requested to ride the team bus to the game. I had to deny their requests. Tiger Don rented his own bus and invited only the elites of the community to ride with him. The only person I allowed to ride with our team was Gerald Davis of the *Lowcountry Times.*

That morning, December 6, 1985, the team assembled in the school cafeteria to be treated with what Coach Hanover had once called the Breakfast of Champions. Every politician, pastor, and business leader of the county showed up for a time to congratulate the team before we began our journey. Middle aged men, who wore their Coosawhatchie letterman's jackets paraded around the cafeteria that morning like they were the ones playing in the game. One of the alumni who had played on the 1968 state championship team, told me, "I love Coach Hanover so much, I would run through a brick wall if he ordered me to do it."

Another younger man who played on the 1976 state championship team said, "If it wasn't for Coach Hanover I would still be hooked on drugs."

Before we finished our breakfast that morning, a surprise guest showed up to speak to the team he loved. When Coach Hanover walked to the front of the cafeteria, everyone stood up and gave him a standing ovation. I introduced him as the man who had built the Coosa football program. Coach Hanover shook my hand and said to the crowd, "I thank you all for the best years of my life, but today is your day. I want all of you players to know one thing. The ride home is much better if you win the game. Don't y'all come home without that damn trophy on the bus."

* * *

Although the players were excited, not a word was said by any of them on the Trailways bus ride to Columbia. Gerald Davis whispered to me, "Frankie told me in the cafeteria that he was so excited to see the big city."

"It's hard to believe that a lot of these kids have never been anywhere too far away from their homes."

Gerald whispered back, "Win or lose, they will always remember this trip. What you're doing for them is special."

Less than two hours later when we slowly approached the home stadium of the University of South Carolina, I stood up, grabbed the Trailways bus microphone, and yelled, "As you can see, we are about to come up to the stadium where we are playing tonight. Coach Morrison, the head football coach for the University of South Carolina has worked it out so that we can walk through the stadium for a few minutes. When this bus stops, I don't want any of you to say a word as we walk out on the field. We'll stay for a few minutes so you can see the place and then I have another treat in store for you."

As the players quietly unloaded from the bus, Gerald Davis punched me on my shoulder and whispered, "Look at their faces. They're so excited."

While we walked on a field of perfection lined and groomed by the famous groundskeeper, Sarge Frye, none of the Coosawhatchie County High School players or coaches had ever seen turf so lush and beautiful. Frankie whispered to me, "They grass is green. Back home our grass is brown this time of year."

I happened to look up and I noticed Coach Morrison standing near the west endzone stadium entrance. He was prohibited from speaking to us by the rules of the NCAA. Coach Morrison waved at me and immediately walked out of view. I laughed to myself when I saw a sign hanging over the entrance gate which was a popular quote from Coach Morrison regarding the stadium which read: "If it ain't swayin'; we ain't playin'."

Fifteen minutes later, we loaded the Trailways bus to go on a scheduled tour of the University of South Carolina campus. Our tour guides were two students named Sherri and Ginger, who met us at the Russell House. They did a good job of explaining the history surrounding the state's oldest university before they guided us on a short walking tour through the middle of campus. When they allowed us to briefly enter the lobby of the Cooper Library, Frankie whispered to me, "Ain't no way one person could ever read all those books."

A few minutes later, we were led through the center of the campus to the historic area called the Horseshoe. While we were there, the entire team was approached by sorority members of Alpha Delta PI. The gorgeous sorority sisters, all dressed in skimpy elf and Santa costumes, were trying to sell Christmas cookies to raise money for their main charity, the Ronald McDonald House. I, and the other assistant coaches, did our best to keep the players under control as we had to politely tell the young ladies that nobody was going to buy any cookies.

After our tour ended, we walked several blocks away and toured the grounds of the South Carolina State House. Another pre-arranged tour guide, who worked at the site, lectured the team with his historical expertise on how Union General William Sherman shelled the State House during the last days of the Civil War. After showing the team the bronze star plaques on the side of the granite building, marking the spots where cannonballs landed, linebacker Doug Pye raised his hand and said, "General Sherman burnt our town to the ground during the Civil War."

The tour guide laughed before replying, "He also burned Columbia to the ground, although he claimed he never gave that order."

After our historical tour, I arranged for us to take a team photo on the steps of the State House. While we stood on the steps waiting for the young photographer named Mark Houde to take the picture, I yelled, "Look out over this place. For the rest of your lives, you will remember the day you stood on the State House steps, knowing you were about to be the kings of Class B, South Carolina high school football."

A few minutes later, all of our assistant coaches handed out sandwiches, snacks, and drinks as the team ate a late lunch on the grounds of the State House. Some of the faithful from Coosawhatchie County that had wandered into town, blew their horns and waved at us as they drove by the State House. Once the last napkins and brown paper lunch bags were picked up and discarded into the trash, I surprised the team when I announced that we would walk down Main Street to go to a theater and watch a movie. Once there, I purchased everyone a ticket, a box of popcorn, and a soft drink. The players were treated to the new movie, *Teen Wolf,* starring Michel J. Fox.

At the conclusion of the movie, we boarded the Trailways bus. Each team member thanked me and my assistant coaches for what we had done. It would be a trip they would remember for the rest of their lives.

* * *

A few hours later we were warming up on the field of Williams-Brice Stadium. I looked around the huge stadium as our team stretched in the East end zone. One of four state title games being played on Friday and Saturday from all of the state's high school classifications, our game was set to start at 6:00 p.m. While I took in all the sights and sounds, I noticed all of the college head coaches sitting together on a reserved row of seats at the fifty-yard line. My thoughts were momentarily disturbed when an Auburn assistant coach walked over to me and said, "Coach Blake, Coach Dye would like for you to walk over to the stands for a minute. He wants to wish you well before the game starts."

I remembered a similar situation earlier in the year with Coach Hanover and Coach Dye. I replied, "You go tell Coach Dye that I'm a little busy right now. As a matter of fact, you tell him that I'm doing the exact same thing that he would do if I asked him to speak with me a few minutes before the Auburn/ Alabama game. I think he will understand."

After we ran a few warm up plays on offense, our entire team stopped what we were doing when we all noticed the Coosawhatchie County Marching Band entering the stadium. When the band struck up the tune of the school's fight song, all of the players and coaches sang along with the band.

* * *

That night, I hardly said a word to the team during my pregame speech. I laughed a few times and even told the players a joke. We were relaxed and ready to play against the very fast Antreville Cougars. When our team ran onto the field that evening, we didn't shout or say a word. We looked like a veteran team who had been there before. While the Antreville team looked fired up, their pregame excitement quickly ended when they fumbled on the first play of the game.

Those who predicted that the game was going to be one of the best state championship games ever played, left that evening very disappointed. Coach Hanover's defensive plan, which loaded up defenders in the box for the run and blitzed with the purpose of confusion for the pass, crushed the Antreville offense. Frankie Lake and our offense ran over the Antreville defense which was outmanned from the start.

By the beginning of the fourth quarter, every player on our team had played at least one or two snaps of the game. With a final score of 48-0, the ending of the game was almost a relief for the coaches from Antreville, who knew in their hearts that we could have scored many more points. When the game officially ended, we shook the hands of our opponents without bragging or saying a word about our win. There was no jumping up and down, wild hand gestures, or any actions perceived to be unsportsmanlike. Our players and coaches conducted themselves in a manner which was as impressive as the game we had played.

When I graciously accepted the state championship trophy from the League Commissioner, I simply shook his hand and said, "Thank you."

The first person I sought out after the game was Shah. She threw her arms around my neck and gave me a big kiss. The next people I found were Coach Hanover and Paige. I gave them both big hugs and said, "Coach, your plan was unbelievable. It worked to perfection."

Before we left the field that evening, Gerald Davis of the *Lowcountry Times* insisted that he take a picture of Coach Hanover and I holding the state championship trophy together. At first Coach Hanover declined until I said, "I'm not leaving here without you doing this. You deserve this more than anybody."

That historical photo still hangs in the gym of Coosawhatchie County High School under the 1985 State Championship Banner.

In my post-game interview with the news media, I gave Coach Hanover all the credit for coming up with a defensive game plan that stymied the opposition. When one reporter suggested that it was me, who had guided the team to an amazing season, I didn't mince words when I said, "Coach Hanover is the blood and soul of our program. We would not have won the game without him. I can't wait to work for him again next season. Our community owes him nothing but gratitude and respect."

Chapter Sixteen

Many people spent their entire paycheck to shoot off fireworks in downtown Coosawhatchie when our team arrived home late that night. Every law enforcement and emergency vehicle in the county had their warning lights flashing when the Trailways bus carrying our team entered the city limits. Our players and coaches were greeted as conquering heroes. The players were all adored like gods when they began to exit the bus in the main parking lot at the school. Some of the players posed for pictures of them holding the state championship trophy. The lights of the stadium were turned on, and the scoreboard was lit up showing the final score of the championship game. Fans from every walk of life greeted the players, who then headed to the locker room to turn in their equipment. Many of those fans shook the hands of their favorite players, sliding them cash without saying a word. Some players received a few dollars while others received much more. Frankie Lake could not carry all the cash he was receiving. His pockets and his letterman's jacket were filled to capacity.

After most of the team had left the locker room, Frankie walked down to the coach's office. He asked me if he could borrow a garbage bag or any type of sack. When I found out that Frankie was asking so he could put away the cash he had received, I walked with him to the locker room to see the cash for myself. I was astonished by the number of twenty and one hundred-dollar bills that were in Frankie's locker. I noticed that many of the bills were stamped with the sports logos of several different universities. After we counted the money, I could not believe that Frankie had collected close to three thousand dollars. I was speechless for a few seconds. I finally asked, "What are you going to do with all this cash?"

Frankie replied, "This ain't my money. This money belongs to the Good Lord. I'm gonna gives it to my church this comin' Sunday morning."

I knew even more than before that Frankie Lake's heart was in the right place. On our ride home that night, I told Frankie that he needed to keep some of the money for himself. Franke laughed at me and said, "I can't keep what ain't mine, Coach."

When I finally arrived home to my sleeping finance, I tried not to wake up Shah. She reached over to me, took hold of my hand and said, "You're the champion. I'm so proud of you."

We talked for a few more minutes before I said, "Let's get married this weekend. We can call in sick this Monday."

"Where would we get married on such short notice? Your old priest from Beaufort has already agreed to marry us. Besides, my parents have already made plans to fly to Charleston. We are not spending hardly any money at all. Both of our parents would be so disappointed. Where is all of this coming from?"

I rolled over toward her, gave her a big hug and said, "I don't know. I'm so tired right now, I can't think straight. You're right. We'll go through the wedding as planned."

* * *

While we were discussing our upcoming wedding, Jimmy and Jerry were having a heated discussion about their prisoner over in Egypt, Georgia. While they sat on the back steps of Jimmy's trailer, Jerry the younger, looked at his brother and asked, "When are we gonna let that coach go?" I know this sounds crazy, but I'm startin' to feel sorry for him. He seems like a really nice guy."

"I hate to tell you this, but the boss says we can't let him go until February."

"What is so special about February?"

"Hell, if I know, but for some crazy reason he wants him fed, taken care of, and cooped up in that huntin' lodge until February. With what he is paying us, I don't care if we keep him forever."

Jerry shook his head and downed the last of his cold beer before saying, "You still have not told me how in the world we are gonna let him go with him knowin' our names."

Jimmy laughed one big laugh before saying, "You let me worry about that small detail. When I get through with him, I promise you that he will never mention our names."

* * *

The next week and a half before Christmas vacation, I was busy entertaining several college head coaches, who came to Coosawhatchie County High School for their formal home visit with Frankie Lake. All of them came knowing that Frankie was opposed to making a visit to their campus. Some of them tried to ramp up their sales pitch by trying to persuade Frankie to go ahead and sign with them. Others did their best to land a commitment of an official visit to their school, while a few of them took another approach all together.

The first coach who came to town on Tuesday was Coach Johnny Majors of the University of Tennessee. Coach Majors was a legend at Tennessee. He had won a National Championship at the University of Pittsburgh in 1976. He and his right-hand assistant, Coach Fulmer were a few minutes early when they arrived at the Lake home. Dressed in a gray tweed sports jacket, black slacks, and a bright orange tie, Coach Majors walked into the house full of Southern charm and exceptional charisma. When he tried to hug Frankie's reluctant mother, James Lake looked at me like Coach Majors was out of his mind. Coach Majors laid it on thick. He was animated and at times emotional. His relentless approach reminded me of a Baptist preacher who was trying to covert a lost soul. His sales technique of asking a question and then answering that same question before anyone could speak was very evident. "Did you know that Knoxville is the safest city in the nation? Why sure you do. Knoxville is also one of the prettiest places you can ever visit. You and Mrs. Lake will love coming up there to see Frankie play."

Coach Majors pressed hard and did it all with the enthusiasm of a starving man who was trying his best to make a sale to avoid a night of hunger. At one point he knelt down on one knee and said, "I'm begging you to make the right decision tonight. Tennessee wants you, son. Don't let the great state of Tennessee down."

Coach Fulmer and I watched as the Master of Southern football recruiting put on a spectacular show. Majors was relentless and kept hammering away until it was clearly evident that Frankie and his family were nowhere near making a final decision. His persistence did pay off as he was able to receive a commitment from James Lake that Frankie would take an official visit to Tennessee in January. It wasn't the victory he came for, but it was a victory worth bragging about as every news media outlet in the Volunteer Nation ran a short story about how Coach Majors was responsible for Frankie Lake making an official visit to Knoxville in January.

The next evening, the Lake family and I were treated beyond our expectations to the down-home sales pitch of Coach Bobby Bowden of Florida State University. When he entered the Lake home, unlike Majors, he hugged the entire family. When he was hugging James Lake, Frankie looked at me and began smiling. Coach Bowden then began his visit by saying, "I don't know where y'all stand with the Lord, but if y'all don't mind I would love to start this meeting with a quick word of prayer."

James cried out, "Amen, brother. Please lead us in prayer."

Coach Bowden bowed his head and closed his eyes before crying out, "Lord, only you know what is best for this young man. We ask you to be with us tonight so that Frankie and his family can make the best decision regarding his future. We love you, Lord, and we can't wait to see you when you return. Amen."

He didn't know it at the time, but Coach Bowden had them sold. If he would have asked, Mr. and Mrs. Lake were ready for Frankie to sign that evening. But Coach Bowden never asked the most important question. He assumed that this was going to be a long recruiting battle so he took his time and tried his best to let them know more about Florida State and himself. His portrayal of himself as a Christian family man explaining that he and his wife Ann had a time raising six children was classic. His stories about how he and Ann robbed Peter to pay Paul when they were first married was priceless. When he concluded the official visit, he hugged all of them again before saying, "I'm sure you have a lot to think about. Once you take a few days and pray about it, I know the Good Lord will make it all clear to you. Obviously, I hope he steers you our way."

Once he left them and headed back to Savannah to catch his flight to Tallahassee, James Lake looked at me and said, "I want Frankie to be with him. That man loves the Lord."

Frankie nodded his head and added, "He is a nice man."

For me, it seemed pretty clear that Florida State would be the one. I told Shah that evening that I was one hundred percent sure that Frankie would become a Seminole. I didn't think that any of the other coaches stood a chance in the recruiting battle for Frankie Lake's soul. Then to my surprise Coach Joe Morrison from the University of South Carolina used a very unique approach the next evening which had the Lake family rethinking what the Good Lord was telling them to do. The former NFL player for the New York Giants was professional, but very relaxed when he asked if he could use their bathroom before the official visit began. Once he finished his bathroom business, the stern looking coach wasted no time when he delved into the business as to why Frankie needed to sign with the University of South

Carolina. He had done his homework on the Lake family when he looked at Frankie and said, "I know you want to help people. Let me tell you how you can best help the people or the organizations you care about the most. The best way you can help others is to give them money. I know that many people believe money is the root of all evil, but I want you to think about how you can help your church or family. Wouldn't it be nice to have the opportunity to give them a large amount of money? Well, son, if you come to the University of South Carolina, I can promise you that I have all the connections you will need to make it in the NFL. I want you to think of the University of South Carolina as the place that will develop you to become a player in the National Football League. Once you make it as a professional football player, you will make millions." Before anyone could say a word, Coach Morrison looked at James Lake and said, "I'm not sure if anyone has told any of you this, but Frankie has all the tools to be a millionaire. I want you to think how that money could benefit your family and your church. Wouldn't it be great to give that money to people who need it the most?"

James Lake perked up saying, "We do need a new sound system at the church now that I think about it."

Coach Morrison never once said a word about education or anything else relating to the University of South Carolina. By saying nothing other than expressing how he could be the one to develop Frankie as an NFL superstar, his approach was mind provoking. He kept hammering away at the potential of Frankie landing big endorsement contracts which had the potential to double or triple his NFL income. Before he left that night, he told Frankie, "I'm the only coach who has all of these professional connections. All these other coaches want you to help them win games for their own glory. When I help you win, we all win?"

I could tell Coach Morrison had hit an exposed nerve. James Lake openly and vocally dreamed about all the good that could be accomplished with future money coming in from the National Football League and corporate endorsements. It was the first time I had heard him say anything about material possessions. After James Lake said a quick prayer, he said, "The Good Lord wants Frankie to be a South Carolina Gamecock so we can give money to the church."

The next day at school, I called Coach Hanover and gave him an update on Frankie's recruitment. Coach Hanover said, "The Lake family is gonna have a hard time makin' a decision. Joe Morrison may have the inside track right now, but there are a few more good programs that will give Frankie and his family their best shot. Didn't you tell me that Coach Paterno is coming this afternoon?'

"Yes, sir. And I can't wait to hear what he has to say."

As soon as I hung up the phone, I heard a knock on the coach's office door. Standing in the doorway was Coach Kenney and the legendary Coach Joe Paterno from Penn State, who had just won the NCAA National Football Championship three years prior.

I wasn't expecting them for quite some time. I kept thinking that they had popped in at a bad time. Coach Paterno cried out in his thick Brooklyn- Italian accent, "Eh, I know we are early kid, but I told Coach Kenney that I wanted to come down here so we could visit with you before we have the official home visit. I always hate it when we are rushed, and I don't have time to talk with you high school coaches. I tell my staff all the time that we need to establish good relationships with you guys. Sometimes we are so busy with recruiting, we overlook our real bread and butter; the high school coaches."

Coach Kenney calmly added, "Coach Paterno never wants us to leave a place without making sure that the recruit's high school coach feels good about what we are doing."

Because of their early arrival, I was somewhat embarrassed with what I had to tell them. "Coach, I hate this but I have one last class that I have to be with today. You and Coach Kenney are more than welcome to sit here or walk around the school until I'm done."

"What subject do you teach?"

"World History."

"Eh, What topic are you covering today?"

"We are about to dive into the French Revolution."

With a sparkle in his eyes he said, "Perfect. I'll be more than honored to speak to your class about the French Revolution."

I started laughing and said, "Thanks, Coach, but–"

"Gees... I do know how to teach a little. For God's sake man, let's go have some fun."

Chapter Seventeen

Dressed in a long sleeve blue button-down shirt, a navy-blue Penn State tie, khaki pants, and black shoes, Coach Paterno put on a show in Room C-107 of Coosawhatchie County High School. I stood in the back of the classroom with Coach Kenney as Paterno delved into the particulars of the French Revolution. About half of the students knew the celebrity coach while the other half had no idea who the man with thick dark eyeglasses was, blistering them with questions about France. He spoke with a funny accent that some of my students had a hard time understanding. He then began lecturing them on the Bourgeois, King Louis XVI, and the Tennis Court Oath.

When he pretended that he was being guillotined by laying down on the top of a desk, he motioned for the entire class to move out of their seats and watch more closely. He jumped up and began giving them all high fives while saying, "History is so much fun."

I could not believe that the famed coach knew as much or more about the French Revolution as I did. By the time class was over, every student had received an autograph from Joe Paterno and words of wisdom about how they needed to listen to their parents.

After the bell rang and my students thanked their guest teacher, Coach Paterno looked at me and asked, "How was that for short notice? Gees, I need to do this more often. I swear, I can't remember when I have had so much fun."

He then sat down in a vacant desk and said, "Let's talk some football."

I received an unexpected education of a lifetime that afternoon as the former quarterback from Brown University explained some of the techniques he was taught back during his playing days in 1949. When he showed me the proper way to secure the football from a direct snap, I wished that I could have been filming his detailed explanation. He then drew up a play on the chalk board that he ran out of the single-wing offense when he was a player at Brown. "Look at the blocking angles. We have been teaching almost the same exact blocking schemes almost thirty-five years later. A lot of young coaches today have no idea."

Then after about forty-five minutes of incredible coaching advice, Paterno asked, "Coach Blake, have you lived, yet?"

I was confused by the question asking, "What did you say, sir?"

Coach Kenney began laughing.

"I asked if you had ever lived?"

Seeing that I didn't know how to reply, Coach Paterno said, "My definition of living is when you drive a station wagon filled with five children and a wife from State College, Pennsylvania all the way to Disney World and back. That, my friend, is what I call living, and I have done it. Until you have experienced my definition of living, you have no idea about the goodness of life."

"I'm about to be married in a few weeks."

"Ah, that's excellent. Whenever you finally have a chance to live, please let me know."

* * *

Later that evening at Frankie Lake's home, Coach Paterno put on another show in front of Frankie and his parents. His approach was much different than what they had heard from the previous two college head football coaches.

He talked about how Frankie, with his good character, could help Penn State become a better institution. He spoke about how the experience of obtaining a college degree was one of the most important things in life. He didn't talk about money and never once mentioned football. His message was centered around what Frankie could do for Penn State as a student, and how he always wanted his players at Penn State to be a student first.

During his dissertation on why Penn State was the best university in the nation, I noticed that James Lake wanted to speak. I interceded saying, "Mr. Lake, do you have something to ask, Coach Paterno?"

Indeed, he did. James asked the famed coach, "Now how is Frankie playin' at your school gonna get him one of those NFL contracts we've been hearin' 'bout?"

Coach Paterno shot back, "Please... for God' sake, man, we have had more players play in the NFL than any other college in the nation. We have a long list of players who are playing in the NFL right now."

Those words had James Lake's attention. He then wanted to know more about Penn State. By the time Coach Paterno left that evening, James Lake and Frankie were sold on Penn State without one moment of prayer.

* * *

On Friday morning, I went to the school early to grade a few papers and to make sure that I was prepared for a full day of scheduling which featured Vince Dooley from the University of Georgia and Bo Schembechler from Michigan coming to visit with Frankie on the same day. On the other side of town, Coach Treadway and Coach Bill Dooley from Virginia Tech were scheduled to visit with Doug Pye and his family. I had made several schedule changes so that I could be at all of the official visits. On top of that, Principal Dean had scheduled an end of the day pep rally to honor the state championship football team.

A few minutes before the afternoon pep rally, Treadway and Bill Dooley showed up at the school much earlier than expected. Treadway was all grins when he confided to me that his mission was accomplished because he had squarely put his sights on Doug

Pye long before anyone else. He told me that his involvement with Frankie Lake eventually became a planned deception so he could have the opportunity to recruit the Pye boy, who he said was a "diamond in the rough." Coach Dooley confirmed their strategy when he said, "Look here, Coach, we knew after a few weeks that it would be hard to snag that Lake kid from the in-state schools if he wasn't gonna make any visits."

Treadway said, "I told you a while back that sometimes half the battle in recruiting is deception. We think the Pye kid will turn into one of our best linebackers before he graduates. I hate to say this but just between us, I think the Lake kid will be a bust. After talking with him, there is no way he is going to stay in college very long."

That afternoon after the quick pep rally, I went to the Pye home for the official visit. Doug's mother Karen, a woman who had a small trailer full of kids and no husband, listened to Coach Dooley for only about ten minutes when she said, "I hate it, but I have an appointment that I have to go to. Now if my boy wants to play with you, let him sign whatever he needs to sign, and he is yours."

Doug Pye signed his commitment papers and unofficially became a Virginia Tech Hokie on a full scholarship pending his final grades and the February National Signing Day.

Coach Treadway later whispered to me, "That was the easiest home visit I have ever been on. We landed who we came for without any problems."

I then drove like a crazy man through the backwoods of Coosawhatchie County. In the nick of time, I made it to Frankie's house the same exact time that Coach Vince Dooley was walking up the front steps. The NCAA National Football Champion Coach of 1980 was dressed in a bright red sports jacket, a white button-down shirt, gray slacks, and a black University of Georgia tie. By far, the Alabama native and Auburn graduate of Irish-

Italian descent was the best dressed coach of them all. There was absolutely no sales pitch involved in what he had to say. He was all business. With a nasal sounding southern accent, he at times seemed a little uncomfortable until he began talking about how he and his staff could make Frankie into the next Herschel Walker. Coach Dooley didn't know it, but James Lake and his wife, Ida Louise had never heard of Herschel Walker. When James Lake finally asked, "Who is this Herschel you keep talkin' 'bout?" Dooley laughed, and looked at me in disbelief.

After he asked Frankie what he wanted to major in, Coach Dooley surrendered his dream of signing the next Herschel Walker when Frankie replied, "Major, Sergeant, or General. It don't matter to me, Coach."

I knew the most professional coach I had ever encountered, began wondering why he had wasted his time in the middle of nowhere. Before he left that evening, Coach Dooley whispered to me, "I know Frankie is one helluva athlete, but God help whoever he signs with. I hate it, but this young man is a lot more academically challenged than I thought. I pray he signs with Clemson or South Carolina. They can have him. Thank you, Coach. Give my best to Coach B.B. and tell him we'll be back to visit next year."

After waving goodbye to Coach Dooley, I walked back inside the Lake home to wait for Coach Schembechler to arrive. I looked and the entire family was sitting on the couch. They had their eyes closed as James Lake led them in prayer. I did my best not to interrupt their family prayer time. During the long prayer, I occasionally peeked at the family, who were all holding hands. I could not believe it when James Lake cried out, "We know he is the most honest coach to visit us. We thank you Lord for showin' us that Georgia is the place for our Frankie."

Once the prayer was over, I asked, "So you liked Coach Dooley?"

James Lake stood up before saying, "Amen to that. Mr. Dooley was all business and he wants Frankie to be the next Herschel. I can sense in my spirit that Georgia is where Frankie needs to be."

At that moment, I knew that James Lake wasn't quite right and that all roads to Frankie's recruitment rested in the prayer life of Frankie's father. I also realized that Frankie was like his father; a man who trusted everyone because he had such a kind heart.

The dogs barking outside signaled the arrival of one of the most successful coaches in college football, Bo Schembechler of the University of Michigan. That evening Bo at first appeared to be tough. He also appeared to be rough around the edges, but he was funny and compassionate. When he told everyone that he had spent a year as a college football assistant coach at Presbyterian College in Clinton, South Carolina in 1954, he made an unexpected connection. It turned out that Ida Louise had cousins who lived and worked at the small college during that same time period. When she told Coach Schembechler the name of her uncle, he almost came to tears before he asked, "Did you say Ronnie Knight? I haven't heard that name in thirty years. Ronnie and I worked together. He and I spent a summer together in a maintenance shop on that little campus. He was in charge of making sure the dorm rooms at Presbyterian College were ready for the arrival of the new students. They had me working with him so I could make some extra cash. That precious man taught me everything I know about carpentry and how to use tools. How in the world is he doing?"

He could hardly understand Ida Louise's slurred speech when she said, "Da stroke gots him. He passed away a few years ago."

After expressing his condolences, Coach Schembechler noticed a carved out wooden duck sitting on the kitchen table. He asked, "Where did you get such a beautiful duck? For Pete's sake it looks just like the real thing."

When James Lake explained how he had carved the duck, Coach Schembechler wanted to see his shed where James produced his fine pieces of art. For the next hour, James Lake showed off pieces of his artwork and instructed Coach Schembechler how to use a lathe for woodworking.

The head football coach from the University of Michigan left that evening after he purchased one hundred dollars' worth of ornamental bowls and depictions of various forms of wildlife. He also left an impression on the Lake family that he was truly a man that could be trusted. It appeared without a doubt after a brief family prayer gathering that Frankie Lake would become a Michigan Wolverine.

Chapter Eighteen

All of the students and faculty members of Coosawhatchie County High School were busy preparing for semester exams during the final week before Christmas vacation. I was still trying to juggle the schedule of the last official recruiting home visits for Frankie Lake. That Monday morning, I was summoned to the Principal's office before the school day began. Once inside the office, I was greeted by Principal Dean and Coach Hanover. Coach Hanover had a big smile on his face when he said, "We called you down here because we have some big news."

A few minutes later, I was surprised to learn that Coach Hanover had officially resigned as the Head Football Coach of Coosawhatchie County High School. Principal Dean also told me that Hanover would be retained as the school's Athletic Director. Coach Hanover then stood up and said, "My first official act of business is to name you as the new head football coach."

Deep in my soul, I was torn about the news. Obviously, I was excited about the possibility of becoming the head coach; however, I hated it that Coach Hanover was finally hanging up his whistle in such an uneventful manner. I tried to talk Coach Hanover into changing his mind. We talked a few more minutes before Coach Hanover finally said, "Look here, Stephen, when the time comes, you know it. I'm sure that when the first game rolls around next year I'll hate it, but in my heart, I'm at peace. My time coaching has come to an end. It's now time for you to lead the boys. You have and will continue to do a great job."

Without an interview or a long drawn out process, I became the new head football coach without any fanfare or news conferences. It was a done deal, and nobody in the community ever objected. Gerald Davis at the *Lowcountry Times* wanted to do an article about me being the first black coach at Coosawhatchie County High School. I knew it was a big deal, but I rejected his idea because I didn't want to overshadow the article that was being done about Hanover, the Korean War hero, who had served his community without ever wanting the lime-light, the once young coach who tried his best to navigate through the uncertain waters of school desegregation; later, a veteran coach who saved his community from ugliness of hate. He's the good man, who gave me the keys to a football kingdom in the middle of nowhere.

That evening, I wanted to go home and share his good news with Shah. Instead, I went to the home of Frankie Lake for another official visit. This night, however, a new person was on hand. When I entered the house, I was somewhat taken back when I saw the pastor of the Jerusalem Fire Baptized Church, Dr. Phillip Osborne. He was sitting at the kitchen table, thumbing through his Bible. After being reintroduced to him, James Lake said, "Sunday mornin' at church the Lord told me that we needed our pastor to be with us to help us make this important decision."

Dr. Osborne immediately spoke up saying, "Coach Blake, the Good Lord is going to direct us where he wants Frankie to go to school next year."

Before I could reply, we heard the dogs barking outside, signaling the arrival of Pat Dye from Auburn University. Coach Dye, who had just been in New York to watch his running back Bo Jackson receive the Heisman Trophy, looked tired when he entered the Lake home. The former assistant coach for Bear Bryant at the University of Alabama, Coach Dye was already a legend as a former All-American lineman at the University of Georgia. Like Vince Dooley and Johnny Majors, Coach Dye was professionally dressed except for the fact that his navy and orange striped Auburn logo tie was hanging loosely around his neck like he had just coached four quarters of football or been in a long poker game. Before Coach Dye could begin his pitch, Dr. Osborne began asking the famous coach questions that were of a religious nature. He first asked Coach Dye if he knew the date of Frankie's baptism. After Coach Dye looked puzzled and didn't respond, Dr. Osborne asked, "Have you been married more than once?"

Coach Dye, at first laughed, thinking his questions were part of a series of planned jokes, until Dr. Osborne asked, "Do you have Bible study with your players?"

Coach Dye immediately looked at me and said, "Is this guy for real or is he just playin' with me?"

James Lake spoke up saying, "Coach Dye, Dr. Osborne is our spiritual adviser."

Coach Dye laughed before saying, "I see. Please forgive me, I didn't know I was comin' to a church meetin' tonight."

When nobody in the room laughed, it shook up Dye, a man who rarely flinched under pressure. It didn't seem to bother him; however, as he went on with his song and dance about Auburn University which in my mind was as plain and simple as anything I had ever heard. When he said, "I can't wait to get home and spend some time with my huntin' dogs while we have a few days off," he opened up a flood gate of conversation for James Lake.

Five minutes later Coach Dye was given a tour of the Lake hunting dogs which were penned up about fifty yards from the house. When he expressed his affection for a Boykin Spaniel named King David, James Lake couldn't resist showing off King David's trained bird dog skills. For the next twenty minutes King David fetched and pointed better than any quail dog that Coach Dye had ever seen. When Dye offered James Lake a thousand dollars for King David, James Lake looked at him and said, "Coach, you know a man can't part with his wife or his best huntin' dog, no matter the offer."

Without discussing football, or Frankie signing with him, Coach Dye left the Lake home that night with a hunch that Auburn was definitely in the hunt for the nation's top prospect. When Dr. Osborne and the Lake family ended a long prayer session a few minutes later, James Lake looked at me and said, "The Good Lord wants Frankie to go to Auburn. Any man who loves bird dogs loves the Lord."

I shook my head and thought that whoever was last, would win the game of Frankie Lake's recruitment.

* * *

On the last day of school at Coosawhatchie County High School before Christmas vacation, I called Gerald Davis of the *Lowcountry Times* and chatted off the record about Frankie's recruitment. I told the veteran sports writer, "This whole process has been the craziest experience of my life. I'm just plain sick and tired of it, and can't wait for it to end."

Gerald laughed. "I have been following high school football for a long time. It's December. A lot of things can happen between now and signing day. I learned long ago to expect the unexpected. Don't be surprised when it happens."

Later at the Lake home, I and the entire Lake family along with Dr. Osborne talked for a few minutes on the front porch while we waited for Coach Danny Ford of Clemson to arrive. It was dusk and we could barely see as a bright orange Cadillac came barreling down the dirt road toward the house. When the car slammed into a pothole filled with water, it almost swerved into a drainage ditch before it went into a power slide. It came within a few feet of hitting a power pole on the side of the yard. A moment later, Ford and his assistant, Coach Miles Aldridge, jumped out of the Cadillac and began walking toward the house. Coach Ford yelled out, "I didn't think we would ever get here. Lord knows y'all live out here deep in the backwoods. I love it."

After the formal introductions, Ford began his spiel by asking Dr. Osborne if he had ever helped give birth to a baby calf. When Dr. Osborne told him he had not, Coach Ford explained that he was late because he had been busy helping one of his cows give birth back on the farm in Clemson. When James Lake asked the already famous coach about his Cadillac, he then said loudly, "I always wanted to drive one of those cars."

Coach Ford insisted that they go for a spin.

James Lake said, "No, sir, but I would like to look under the hood."

While we all went outside and looked over the 1984 Cadillac Deville with its 4.1 V8 engine, Coach Ford untucked his white Clemson shirt from his gray slacks. After starting up the car, Coach Ford insisted that Dr. Osborne sit behind the wheel. Once he was seated, Coach Ford yelled, "Y'all get in and let's take this baby for a ride."

All of us piled into the car while Ida Louise walked back into the house. For the next thirty minutes, Dr. Osborne, James Lake, and Frankie all drove the fancy car through the back roads in the most rural areas of Coosawhatchie County. I held on for dear life as Coach Ford kept telling James Lake to gun it. He then cried out, "I always say, if you can't have a little fun, life is not worth living."

After finally arriving back at the Lake home, Coach Ford asked, "I hate to ask this, but do y'all have anything to eat or drink? Coach Aldridge and myself didn't have time to eat any supper. A peanut butter sandwich or a bowl of grits would be fine. I don't want to put y'all out."

James Lake cried out, "Frankie, go fetch some eggs."

Ten minutes later, Ida Louise was busy frying up some canned Spam and boiling water for a big pot of grits while Coach Ford was busy frying up some scrambled eggs. While they cooked together, Ford joked with Ida Louise that he was the better cook. I was amazed at how down to earth Coach Ford and Coach Aldridge interacted with the Lake family.

Before our meal was over, Coach Ford seemed like he was just another family member coming by for a visit with his best friend, Coach Aldridge. Ford talked about his farm and he talked about fishing. He talked about everything except football and the recruitment of Frankie Lake. Before he and Coach Aldridge walked out of the Lake home, Coach Ford stopped and asked Dr. Osborne to pray for them to have safe travel back to Clemson. As Dr. Osborne prayed an eloquent prayer, I peeked at Coach Ford who was smiling a big smile. I knew without a doubt that I had witnessed one of the best in the business do what he did best. Without any big prayer meeting later that night, James Lake declared to me that the Good Lord wanted Frankie Lake to attend Clemson University.

* * *

That next Saturday afternoon my father stood next to me in a small Catholic chapel in Summerville; a small town not far from Charleston. He, along with a few family members and friends, watched as Shah and I officially became man and wife. Seated next to Paige and Coach Hanover was Frankie Lake. During the service, Frankie walked up to the front of the chapel and sang his heart out without the accompaniment of any musical instruments or sound system. Frankie's performance that afternoon was his wedding gift to us. It was spectacular.

At the very back of the chapel, four uninvited guests stood like they were hired security guards. They watched the number one recruit in the nation sing his heart out. Coach Treadway, Coach Fulmer, Coach Kenney, and Coach Aldridge had all met at the Charleston airport and driven together to attend my wedding. Although I knew that they were present for business purposes, when I saw them, I smiled, hoping that on some level, I had made friendships with this group of men that would last much longer than one football season.

During our small reception, Hanover whispered to me, "You have a good time this weekend, but when you get back home, we need to talk."

I whispered back, "Coach, you can't leave me hanging like that. What's wrong?"

"You're not going to believe it, but Frankie informed Paige that he wants to take an official visit to the University of Miami in January."

I whispered loudly, "What the hell?"

"I said the same thing. When I asked Frankie where this came from he told me that he had an older cousin who talked to his father last night. Frankie said the next thing he knew was that they wanted him to visit the University of Miami. Poor Frankie is scared to death."

Chapter Nineteen

We stayed in a nice bed and breakfast in downtown Charleston, but our honeymoon was short and sweet. While we strolled around the Battery of Charleston on Sunday afternoon, I informed Shah everything I knew about Frankie Lake's recruitment. As we walked by the famous Rainbow Row where we first fell in love, Shah said, "It sounds to me that nobody is really listening to what Frankie wants. You need to have a talk with his parents when we go home."

I squeezed her hand in a loving way and said, "You don't know his father. He is good man, but I don't think he would welcome my opinion. He sure hasn't this far in the process. I don't know what to say other than I hate all of this for Frankie because he is such a good young man. The last thing I want is for Frankie to come out of this experience jaded or emotionally harmed in any way."

* * *

While we were taking in the sights of historic Charleston, Coach Jaden Geiger was trying his best not to give up all hope of ever seeing his friends and family again. Although he had not been harmed, or mistreated in any way, he was bored out of his mind. As each day of his captivity passed, he found himself looking forward to the brief contact of his captors. They had been careful not to say much around him, but each time they showed up, Coach Geiger did his best to have a conversation with them. If it wasn't for their visits, he probably would have gone insane. The solitude was excruciating as his mind wandered continuously. Each day he looked for ways to escape or plotted on how he could overtake his captors. Those thoughts alone served him well as he continuously planned and schemed the day he would escape.

On this particular day he found out a vital bit of information which gave him the knowledge of where he was located. That afternoon when the two brothers came to bring him lunch, Coach Geiger told them that he wasn't going to eat again until they let him go. He said, "I have no reason to live anymore."

Brother Jerry asked, "What makes you say that foolishness?"

"Because you're lying to me. You're going to kill me."

Jerry shook his finger at him and said, "I swear we are not going to kill you. Our boss came to Egypt this mornin'..."

The other brother, Jimmy yelled, "Shut up Jerry!"

Geiger asked, "You have me locked up all the way in Egypt? Are you guys with the CIA?"

Jerry laughed. "No, stupid. You is in Egypt, Georgia, and we don't work for no CIA."

Jimmy had just about had it with his dumb brother. "Why can't you keep your big mouth shut?"

"Well, at least I ain't as stupid as him. He thinks he's in the big Egypt. You know, the one that has people with jewels in their foreheads."

"That's India, you idiot; not Egypt."

"India, Egypt, they are all the same. Savannah River, Altamaha River, they are all the same to me."

Later, during their daily walk around the swamp, Geiger intensified his planning and scheming.

* * *

The day after Christmas, 1985, I drove over to talk to James Lake. Ida Louise answered the door and told me that James was working in the shed with Frankie. I didn't mean to interrupt their woodworking, but I needed to find out more about why the University of Miami was now in the hunt with Frankie's recruitment. I listened intently as James Lake explained that his cousin, who lived in Florida, thought that the new head football coach at the University of Miami, a man by the name of Jimmy Johnson, was a good guy. I was visibly frustrated when I said, "I don't mean any disrespect, Mr. Lake, but this has gotten way out of hand. During our last conversation you were sold on Frankie going to Clemson. Why the change of heart?"

"I like them all. I think the Lord will reveal to us where Frankie needs to go to school."

Knowing that it was going to be hard to argue with the Lord, I simply said, "I understand, but–"

"Just make the arrangements for Frankie to go to Miami."

* * *

Two days later, I was finally able to contact Coach Johnson on the phone. After I explained to him that Frankie Lake wanted to make an official visit to the University of Miami, Johnson, who had played at the University of Arkansas as a defensive lineman on the 1964 National Football Championship team, cried, "That's fantastic. Our people here have been expecting your call."

"What people?"

"You know. Our scouting and recruiting folks."

I wanted to know more, but Coach Johnson sidestepped my questions. "Our people will make all the arrangements."

"I don't think you understand. This young man is special–"

Coach Johnson interrupted me saying, "Why sure he is. We already know that."

For several minutes I tried everything I could do to make Coach Johnson realize that Frankie traveling to Miami was going to be an undertaking that he and his staff could not possibly understand.

Finally, Coach Johnson said, "We've seen it all. Go worry about something else. We'll take real good care of Frankie when he arrives."

* * *

It didn't take twenty-four hours for Coach Phillip Fulmer of the University of Tennessee to give me a call. When he began to voice his disappointment that Frankie had already booked a visit to the University of Miami, I asked, "How did you find this out?"

"Word travels fast in the college coaching profession."

I tried hard to explain that I had nothing to do with the shocking official visit to Miami. Coach Fulmer didn't care. All he wanted was a definite date in January for an official visit to the University of Tennessee. Finally, I caved in and secured a date for an official visit to the University of Tennessee without talking to Frankie or the Lake family. On top of that, Coach Fulmer made sure that Tennessee had their official visit scheduled before the visit to the University of Miami.

The next day, I began to pay for my blunder by having to answer to all of the other college coaches who wanted in on an official visit from Frankie Lake. Even Henry Bozzard called and wanted to know when Frankie was going to take an official visit to Clemson. Tiger Don called and said, "If he needs a ride, tell him I'll be glad to take him to Clemson."

When the mayor of Coosawhatchie, Gamecock Gene, called me he said, "You just let me know what I need to do to help Frankie make his way over for a visit to the University of South Carolina."

I succumbed to the pressure and scheduled official visits without consulting anyone.

It wasn't until a few days later that I learned from Coach Hanover that Frankie could only take five official visits per the rules of the NCAA. I looked at my boss and said, "I have screwed this up. I have overbooked."

Hanover shook his head and said, "Don't worry about it. Something tells me this will work itself out."

The week that school started back at Coosawhatchie County High School in January, I informed the Lake family that Frankie would definitely be flying to the University of Tennessee and the University of Miami the next week. James Lake wasn't happy about the Tennessee trip until I reminded him that he had made a commitment to Coach Johnny Majors. I said, "The only reason I booked the visit to Tennessee was because I knew you were a man of your word."

James Lake nodded his head in affirmation and didn't reply. A few minutes later James Lake informed me that he would not be able to fly with Frankie for the visit to Knoxville. I looked at Frankie and said, "Don't worry, Coach Hanover or I'll go with you."

Hanover opted out when I told him that he needed to go with Frankie. He simply said, "I hate flyin'. The last time I was on a plane was when I came home from the Korean War. I ain't never gonna fly again."

* * *

The next Friday afternoon, Coach Fulmer greeted Frankie and me at the Savannah Airport. Frankie was so nervous and scared, he could not say a word. Coach Fulmer could not help but noticed that Frankie was carrying a nice-looking suitcase, but that I was empty handed. Fulmer asked, "So I see Frankie is prepared, where is your suitcase, Coach Blake?"

I simply replied "We packed together."

The truth of the matter was that when I picked up Frankie for the flight, he had his clothes stuffed in a plastic garbage bag. When Frankie revealed that his family didn't own a suitcase, it broke my heart. In the parking lot of the Savannah Airport we transferred Frankie's clothes from the garbage bag into my suitcase before we met Coach Fulmer.

As we walked across the airport's tarmac toward the Tennessee Learjet, I was enamored by the big orange T logos on the tail and door of the impressive looking plane. Frankie on the other hand, looked like he was about to be sick.

After the door to the Learjet was closed and we were all seated, a big screen at the front of the jet began rolling down from the ceiling. The lights in the cabin of the Learjet dimmed as if we were in a theater. A projector from the back of the jet began playing a film that had been prepared for our flight. Accompanied with music and top of the line industry graphics, the University of Tennessee had prepared a movie for and about Frankie Lake. The movie title flashed across the screen reading: *The Lake Effect.* The soundtrack associated with this professionally made film included the tunes of Frankie's favorite gospel songs. Because of the film, the darkness of the cabin, and the sleek handling of the Learjet, Frankie and I never knew that we had departed from the Savannah Airport. Using Coosawhatchie County High School game film from the previous season, the graphics people at the University of Tennessee were able to transfer some of Frankie's greatest runs of the season into scenes where Frankie was wearing a Tennessee jersey and helmet. How they were able to accomplish this cinematic feat was mind boggling. Showing clips of Frankie playing in front of one hundred thousand yelling fans at Neyland Stadium was ingenious. All that I could think about was that someone at the University of Tennessee had spent a lot of time making this incredible film.

An hour later, right as the *Lake Effect* movie was ending with a scene of Frankie holding up the National College Football Championship Trophy while wearing a Tennessee football uniform, we landed in Knoxville; not believing what we had witnessed or how quickly we had arrived.

The opening of the Learjet's door signaled the last time that weekend that I would see Frankie. When we began walking down the steps of the Learjet, we were greeted by a line of cheerleaders and band members who were playing and singing the Tennessee fight song, "Rocky Top." Students holding printed orange and white signs which read: We LOVE YOU FRANKIE cheered as we walked through a long human tunnel which was shaped in the form of the letter "T." Once we exited the line of cheerleaders, band members, and students, Frankie was ushered away in one direction by a couple of graduate assistants while Coach Fulmer escorted me in the opposite direction. Because of the deafening noise surrounding us, I could not communicate with Fulmer until we were inside of a white, University of Tennessee van driven by a graduate student, who worked in the athletic department.

I yelled at Fulmer, "Where in the hell is Frankie?"

He turned around from the front seat and replied, "Coach, don't worry about Frankie. He is having the time of his life. The best thing you can do is try to relax. I assure you that Frankie Lake is in good hands."

Chapter Twenty

After dropping me off at my hotel room, Coach Fulmer told me that I needed to be down in the lobby in one hour so that we could all go to dinner. I assumed that Frankie would be coming to the hotel room or meeting us at the dinner. Nothing about that was ever said, but it had definitely been implied.

A little more than an hour later and a few miles away from the main campus, Fulmer and I were seated at the Ye Olde Steak House. Coach Majors was already waiting for us while he sipped on a beverage and jotted down notes in a small black notebook. I was in awe of the man who appeared to be more than a football coach. He congratulated me on winning the state championship and talked to me like I was one of his best friends. His down-home Southern charm made him seem like I was speaking to a close relative.

After congratulating Coach Majors on his team's thrashing of the University of Miami in the Sugar Bowl a week earlier, and winning the Southeastern Conference title, I immediately asked, "Is someone bringing Frankie here, or is he eating somewhere else?"

Fulmer said, "He's eating with the rest of the team at our Training Table on campus. If truth be told, the food is so good there, we might want to join them."

Coach Majors laughed and added, "That's one thing I take pride in. I want our players to have the best when it comes to nutrition."

"What time do you think Frankie will be checking in with me at the hotel?

"Didn't Coach Fulmer tell you?"

"Tell me what?"

"Forgive the miscommunication, but Frankie will be staying in a dorm room with several of the captains on our squad. Now, don't worry, those young men will take care of him and treat him like he's royalty."

I was anything but happy, but calmed down after Fulmer said, "Trust me. We have this down to a science. Our people do a great job of hosting and making our recruit's time here very special."

After dinner, Fulmer insisted that I accompany him to the University of Tennessee's football offices so that we could watch some game film and talk football. While I watched Fulmer draw X's and O's all over a chalkboard in his office, I couldn't help but worry about Frankie. I knew the stories associated with the recruitment of players at the large universities. I could not concentrate as Coach Fulmer spoke about blocking angles and how he taught his linemen to step with short, six-inch power steps. My mind began racing when I imagined Frankie being introduced to girls who were looking to find the next college superstar with the potential to become a millionaire.

Several times as if it was planned, each assistant coach at the University of Tennessee came into Fulmer's office and introduced themselves to me. Every one told me how impressed they were that I had won the state championship at Coosawhatchie. They also told me that they would be so excited if Frankie decided to become a Volunteer. With my ego being stroked every few minutes, I all but forgot that Frankie was on his own in Knoxville.

During our film session, Fulmer pointed out various technical errors of a few of Tennessee's botched plays that had been committed in the only game they had lost earlier in the season against the University of Florida. He said, "Thank God we were able to fix those mistakes. Our offensive line improved each game after that. Even with all of the improvements, nobody gave us much of a chance against Miami in the Sugar Bowl. I don't tell this to everybody, but it sure was a lot of fun whipping Coach Johnson and that bunch. Thanks to our defense and our quarterback Daryl Dickey, we were able to pull off the upset."

It was way past midnight when I finally returned to my hotel room. I made a long-distance phone call to Shah. At first, she was aggravated that I had not called earlier until I explained my dilemma regarding Frankie. She did her best to reassure me that Frankie would be fine, but in the back of her mind, she also worried about the most innocent and caring young man she had ever met. Then after we hung up, and before I began to doze off, I realized that Frankie had my suitcase with all of my clothes. It infuriated me that I was going to be stuck in a Knoxville hotel room having to wear the same clothes the next day.

* * *

Early the next morning, I woke up to the banging on my hotel room door. I looked out of the peep hole and couldn't believe that Coach Fulmer was standing on the other side of the door. I glanced at my wrist watch and noticed it was 7 a.m. When I opened the door, Coach Fulmer was standing there with my suitcase. He cried out, "Sorry about your luggage. We let Frankie take what he needed. Take a shower, and change. We have plans today."

While I showered, Coach Fulmer sat on the side of the bed and made several phone calls. He was still talking to another coach by the time I finished with my shower. As I started dressing, he hung up the phone, and said, "Just for your information, Frankie is having a good time. He's going on an academic tour of the campus. I think the President of the University and Coach Majors are eating breakfast with him right now. My grad assistant told me that Frankie will be on a pre-arranged phone call with that new TV talk show star, Oprah or something like that. Evidently, she is an UT alumnus, who our people use from time to time. Our alumni association is pretty big."

* * *

On that cold blustery morning in Knoxville, Coach Fulmer taught me how to play an indoor game of racquetball where we talked about everything except football. When I asked him if he ever wanted to be a college head football coach, he bent over, picked up the ball, and said, “There is only one head coaching job in the world that I would ever want. I’m a Tennessee boy.”

We showered after the game and Fulmer gave me some UT gear. My sweat pants and shirt were a little too large, but I didn’t mind. He then took the time to give me a tour of the campus before we ate lunch. After a long lunch at the UT Training Table, we ended up back at the Tennessee Football Offices.

Timed to perfection, Coach Majors called over an intercom in Coach Fulmer’s office, “Bring Coach Blake in here. We have some good news... Frankie wants to be a Volunteer!”

When we entered the big office of Coach Majors, Frankie was sitting in a faded orange colored chair while Coach Majors was standing behind his desk. I asked Frankie, “Are you –”

Coach Majors interrupted. “All he has to do now is sign this commitment paper and we’ll be done.”

I asked Coach Majors, “What exactly did Frankie say?”

Coach Majors replied, “I asked him if he wanted to be a Volunteer and he said, sure. Coach Blake, in my business that means he wants to be with us. Technically, one could say that’s a verbal commitment.”

I suspected that Frankie didn’t know what he had been asked. I looked at Coach Majors and asked if I could have a few minutes with Frankie alone. While Coach Majors and Coach Fulmer waited outside of the office, I made Frankie repeat everything that had been said.

After telling me the entire conversation between him and Coach Majors, Frankie finally said, “All I know is he asked me to volunteer. I don’t know why he got all excited when I said, "sure" cause back home I always volunteer when Pastor Osborne asks me to help out in da church."

I asked Frankie, "Do you know what the mascot is for this university?"

Frankie quickly asked, "What is a mascot?"

"A mascot is the nickname for the team. Back home, our school's mascot is the Crocodiles. What do you think the mascot is for the University of Tennessee?"

Frankie looked around the room for a few seconds before asking, "Is it an orange or a grapefruit?"

I laughed before saying, "I'm not sure. Now that you say that, their colors do look similar to the color of a grapefruit." I paused for a moment before asking the most important question, "Frankie, do you want to come to school here and play football?"

Frankie asked, "Will you be mad at me if I say, no?"

"Why do you think I'll be mad with you?"

"Because I think you like it here."

"What makes you say that?"

"Because one of their coaches said you were havin' a lot of fun last night. He said I would be botherin' you when I told him that I wanted to spend the night with you."

Frankie's words made my heart melt. I then asked, "Do you or do you not want to come here and play football?"

Frankie replied, "No, sir. Some of the girls tried to attack me. They tried hard to kiss me and put their hands all over my body after begging me to drink beer. I don't think the Lord wants me at this school. I would never get any of my school work done at this place."

I asked, "Did any of the coaches, players, or anyone else give you money or promise you anything else?"

"No, sir. They were all nice to me. I like it here at this school, but these pretty Tennessee girls like me too much."

While Frankie waited out in the lobby of the University of Tennessee, I tried very hard to make Coach Majors understand the confusion over what Frankie told him. I could tell that Coach Majors was a little aggravated, but after a few minutes he told me that he understood. He then laughed at me and said, "I know that I'm not crazy."

To his credit, Coach Majors was a true professional. Because I thought so much of him and Coach Fulmer I didn't want to disappoint them. I then conveniently told them that Frankie would not commit until signing day. "Frankie wants his decision to be a secret. He believes that it will be to his financial advantage to wait until signing day. However, I'll tell you that he appreciates what you have done for this visit. He told me that this visit has made a lasting impression that he will never forget."

My words were not exactly what they wanted to hear, but they were enough to keep UT in the hunt for a prized recruit they desperately wanted. A few minutes later, Coach Majors walked out of his office, gave Frankie a big hand shake and said, "We can't wait for you to be a Volunteer."

Frankie smiled and said, "You don't have to wait long, because I love being a volunteer."

Coach Johnny Majors winked at Coach Fulmer and said, "Signing day is going to be special this year."

Chapter Twenty-One

Frankie and I flew by ourselves on the Learjet back to Savannah. Frankie told me that he didn't want to visit the University of Miami or any of the other universities that were scheduled. He didn't want to disappoint his father, but he didn't like flying and he certainly didn't like spending the night with people he didn't know. I did my best to explain that no matter where he decided to go to school, he would have to be around people he didn't know.

Frankie looked at me and said, "That ain't so. I know Doug, and I could go to school with him at Virginia Tech. Doug is my friend, and he won't let anyone make fun of me."

I thought to myself that Frankie might not be well versed in the world of academia, but he was a lot smarter than I gave him credit for. "That's the most intelligent thing I have heard from you in quite some time. Is Virginia Tech your choice?"

For the first time since we boarded the Learjet, Frankie smiled and said, "I want to go wherever Doug goes."

"You don't even have an official visit planned with Virginia Tech."

"That's ok with me. I don't want to take any more trips. I'm ready to sign with them as soon as I can."

On our ride from the Savannah airport to Coosawhatchie, I thought about this new revelation while Frankie sang several of his favorite gospel songs. I didn't know how this news was going to be received by James Lake and I certainly didn't know if Virginia Tech even wanted Frankie after my last conversation with Coach Treadway and Coach Dooley. As I pondered over this delicate situation, I finally spoke up and said, "Frankie, give me a few days to work all this out. Let's keep this a secret until I have time to figure out the best way to approach your father and the coaches at Virginia Tech. We don't want to upset anyone."

"Whatever you say, Coach."

Later that evening, I told Shah everything that had occurred on Frankie's visit to the University of Tennessee. "It sounds like you're in a pickle. I hate this for you, but I hate it more for Frankie. That poor young man is stuck between a rock and hard place."

A few minutes later, I called Coach Hanover and explained the situation to him. He began laughing. "Out of the mouth of babes... or should I say, the Babe himself." He paused and took a deep breath. "Coach, the first thing I would do is find out from Virginia Tech if their offer is still on the table. You and I would look like the biggest jackasses in Coosawhatchie County if you, me, or Frankie announced that he wanted to attend Virginia Tech and Virginia Tech didn't want him. The worst scenario for Frankie would be if Virginia Tech snubbed him. The rest of the colleges might do the same because they thought Virginia Tech found out somethin' 'bout Frankie that they didn't know."

"I agree, but what do I tell James Lake about Frankie not wanting to travel to Miami or any of the other schools?"

"Don't say anything right now. Let me think about it this weekend. You try to get some news from Virginia Tech, and we'll come up with a plan of attack on Monday."

I wasted no time trying to call Coach Treadway. After three busy signals later, I decided to try one last time before Shah gave me a dirty look and said, "It can wait until the morning."

* * *

Sunday morning brought a cold front into Coosawhatchie County that had the local duck hunters praising the Lord while the rest of the population shivered and turned up their heaters. I woke up early that morning when Shah had to use the bathroom. When she returned to the bed she whispered, "I turned up the heater, but this house is colder than any place I have been in New Jersey."

Once I rearranged the covers of the bed, the phone began ringing. I looked at the radio clock next to the bed and yelled, "Who in the world is calling at 6:30 in the morning?"

"Good morning," a chipper sounding Coach Danny Ford yelled over the phone.

"Good morning, Coach. What can I do for you this morning?"

"Not one thing. I wanted to call to find out if Tennessee offered Frankie a car or you a new job."

"Neither."

Coach Ford laughed before saying, "That's good news. How are you and Shah?"

"We are doing good."

"Great. I have to run now. I can't wait to see you and Frankie in a few weeks. Have a great day."

I looked over at Shah and said, "That was Coach Ford from Clemson. He might be the hardest working head football coach in the country."

"He must be a nut to call so early in the morning."

The phone rang again. This time it was Coach Joe Morrison from the University of South Carolina. He wanted to know if Frankie needed a ride to Columbia for his official visit. Right after his call, Coach Dye from Auburn called. He wanted to talk about the weather and bird hunting. A few minutes after Coach Dye's call, Coach Paterno and Coach Jimmy Johnson both called, making sure that Frankie was still on board for their official visits.

Shah, who had eaten breakfast and started reading the Sunday paper said, "These people don't seem to have much of a life. I'm not sure you should ever consider becoming a college football coach. All they do is talk on the phone, travel to God knows where, and they seem to be away from their families a good portion of their time. They may be compensated for their long hours, but it does not seem worth it to me."

I agreed with her and then picked up the phone and called Coach Treadway at his home in Virginia. While I dialed the number, I told Shah, "I hate to bother him, but this can't wait."

Coach Treadway didn't seem bothered that his only day off was being interrupted by a high school coach from the Lowcountry of South Carolina. I was desperate. While I explained the situation regarding Frankie Lake, I prayed that my new friend, Coach Treadway, would tell me what I wanted to hear. He didn't. Instead Treadway was honest. He told me that everyone knew that Frankie was a great athlete, but he personally didn't think Frankie would pan out on the academic side of things. In the end, he explained that he wanted to help me out, but Virginia Tech had no desire to sign Frankie. I almost came to tears before saying, "I don't know what to do."

Coach Treadway was compassionate when he said, "I think I have a solution to your problem. I promise that we'll not say a word about this on our end. You have my word that none of this will be leaked to the news media. We have just as much or more to lose as you do. Can you imagine how it would look if everyone knew that we took a pass on the nation's number one recruit? We would be laughed out of the state of Virginia. You tell Frankie in a discrete way that he didn't meet our school's academic requirements. Believe me, he will not say a word about it to anyone."

* * *

Monday morning, I picked up Frankie for school. Before he had shut the car door, the greatest athlete in Coosawhatchie County looked at me and asked, "When you gonna tell my Pops 'bout Virginia?"

Before we had reached the end of his dirt road, Frankie was in tears after I gave him the bad news. He began sobbing. I put on the brakes and talked to Frankie for several minutes. I had never seen Frankie cry. At one point of the conversation, I tried to laugh it off and explain that it wasn't meant to be. Frankie was emotionally crushed. He said, "If I can't go with Doug to Virginia, I don't know which school I want to go to."

"Frankie, if I were you, I would pick one of the in-state schools. That way you don't have to be so far away from your family."

Frankie didn't respond.

"Which one do you think you like better, Clemson or South Carolina?"

"Whichever one says Doug can come with me."

* * *

Later that morning, I informed Coach Hanover about the situation. After listening to what he called the "soap opera," he said that Frankie's recruitment could not be pawned to entice a school to sign Doug Pye. "This is a big mess. It looks like I'm going to have to meet with Frankie and his father to get this resolved before we find ourselves in another media circus."

That afternoon, I rode with Hanover and Frankie to discuss the situation with James Lake and Ida Louise.

Coach Hanover deftly explained the situation. James and Ida Louise seemed stunned. Frankie sat still next to his mother. He cried the entire time and only nodded when James Lake asked him if what Hanover said was true; he nodded his head.

Hanover kept the conversation on track. "Frankie has several options, but Doug Pye is out of the picture. I don't care where Frankie goes to school, but y'all need to decide."

Ida Louise, who usually kept quiet now found her voice. "James, all this college talk has turned our family upside down. I want it to stop today, right now. Wherever Frankie decides to go is up to him. No more prayin' and no more plans. This is Frankie's choice."

James Lake shook his head in acknowledgment.

Frankie said, "I'll let everyone know on signing day."

* * *

It was a gross understatement to say that Coach Jimmy Johnson of of Miami, and all of the other coaches who had scheduled an official on-campus visit with Frankie Lake were very upset when Coach Hanover called and told them that Frankie's recruitment had ended. They all tried to persuade him to change Frankie's mind, but the old salty veteran cut all of them off at the knees saying, "It's over. Frankie done made up his mind. He will let the world know his final decision in a few weeks."

When Tiger Don and Henry Bozzard paid Hanover a visit he listened before telling them that Frankie's recruitment was none of their business. Both men did their best to persuade him to intervene, but of course he didn't budge.

Coach Ford from Clemson University called me and asked, "Is there anything we can do on our end to get Frankie up here on a visit?"

"Coach, the boy is an emotional train wreck. He just wants to be left alone."

When Gamecock Gene showed up at Coach Hanover's office, unannounced, he wasn't able to utter three words before Hanover cut him off saying, "There is nothing you can say or do. Have a nice day."

* * *

Although Hanover and I hoped that such finality would make the colleges and universities leave Frankie alone, we were sadly mistaken. Once again, the assistant coaches descended on Coosawhatchie hoping to somehow have the opportunity to persuade the nation's number one undecided recruit. When a national recruiting magazine published an intriguing article about Frankie, the recruiters went wild. The article mentioned that an unnamed source close to the family was quoted as saying that the recruitment was "wide-open" and that Frankie had not decided.

Head Football Coach Jimmy Johnson from Miami sent his entire coaching staff; one at a time for the next two weeks. Coach Aldridge from Clemson was the first person at the high school each day during the last week of January. Coach Kenney from Penn State, stood at the edge of Frankie's dirt road every morning for five days straight.

Cards, telegrams, balloons, candy, and flowers were sent to Coosawhatchie County High School on behalf of Frankie Lake from all over the nation. Coach Hanover and I spent a great deal of our time fielding questions from college coaches and reporters. The buzz around Coosawhatchie was electric. Everyone speculated, some thought they knew which school Frankie would choose, while others made boastful predictions claiming they had insider knowledge about which school Frankie had chosen.

Frankie Lake and his family soon became prisoners at their own home. They could not leave without someone watching their every move. Reporters and graduate assistant college football coaches did their best to catch Frankie alone. They pestered close family and friends. When a sports reporter was found inside a restroom at Coosawhatchie County High School, hiding in a stall to ambush Frankie with questions, Principal Dean put Coosawhatchie High School on media lockdown.

While the circus of Frankie Lake's recruitment continued to dominate the news and gossip of the town, everyone in the Lowcountry was shocked two weeks before National Signing Day when a duck hunter riding down the Coosawhatchie River in his boat, caught a glimpse of something which looked strange and out of place. When he maneuvered his boat next to a small stump near the bank, he almost fell overboard when he realized that what he was looking at was a badly decomposed human torso caught between two cypress trees. Once the torso was recovered from the river, authorities used divers in hopes of finding the other missing body parts. After two days of dragging and diving they found nothing. With only a badly burned torso of what authorities believed to be that of a young African American male, many assumed that it was the body of Coach Jaden Geiger. After family members and the University of South Carolina officials were notified, Sheriff Varnadore of Coosawhatchie County announced the news to the public.

Chapter Twenty-Two

While his family grieved over the horrific news and began making funeral arrangements, Coach Geiger took the gamble of his life when he decided the time had come to flee his captors. After many days of planning, he made his move when the brothers took him for his daily walk next to the edge of the swamp. Uncuffed, he was able to strike up a conversation with Jerry, who had become increasingly chatty over the past few days. While Jerry told him that the weatherman said it was going to be a little warmer next week, Geiger saw that Jimmy was walking with his pistol in his holster.

He had noticed that over the past few days, Jimmy had not been holding his pistol like he had been doing the first days he was allowed to walk outside. As they approached the long wooden dock which led into the thick swamp, Coach Geiger stopped, bent over and pretended to tie his tennis shoe as he had planned. While Jerry kept rambling about the weather, Coach Geiger quickly turned and launched himself like a human torpedo. Jerry was stunned when Coach Geiger hit him in the chest with a forearm flipper that he had learned during his days as a football player and coach. Jerry fell backwards and knocked down his brother like dominoes falling on each other. Geiger sprang to his feet and ran down the wooden dock like he had never run before. Before Jimmy could pull out his pistol, Coach Geiger dove into the swamp waters, and began swimming like a man possessed. In between his thrashing through the cold January waters, Coach Geiger could hear Jerry yelling for him to come back. He also heard Jimmy firing his pistol. A couple of bullets flew right beside him. How he made it across a twenty yard stretch of open water was amazing. How he was able to flee Egypt was almost biblical.

For the next few hours in a swampy forest near the Turkey Branch Baptist Church, Coach Geiger waded through pools of muddy water, and fought his way through thick areas which reminded him of a jungle. Jimmy and Jerry launched a boat and tried to find their escapee. By nightfall, Jimmy and Jerry were forced to make a phone call to their boss letting him know that Coach Geiger had escaped.

While that was happening, Geiger shivered and huddled under the branches of a small Red Cedar and a medium- sized Magnolia tree in the middle of the forest. He prayed that he would not freeze to death, that his captors would not find him, and that he would be able to make it to civilization.

The next afternoon after trudging through the thick forest, he was lost, tired, freezing, and hungry. He somehow stumbled onto Georgia State Highway 21, only a few miles away from the Georgia- South Carolina state line. He waited for hours until he was luckily able to flag down a Georgia State Trooper.

* * *

While an African Methodist Episcopal minister in downtown Raleigh, North Carolina was giving a most eloquent eulogy for Jaden Geiger, a member of the South Carolina Highway Patrol's special detail unit walked into the church, and whispered to University of South Carolina President James Holderman that Coach Jaden Geiger had been found alive. President Holderman whispered to Coach Joe Morrison, "These people are going to be shocked when they find out that Coach Geiger has risen from the dead."

The news media went into a full-fledged frenzy back in South Carolina while Coosawhatchie County Sheriff Varnadore didn't hesitate to place the blame for the misidentification of a burned torso on the Coroner of Coosawhatchie County, Manfred Butterfield. When the news media found out that Manfred lacked any medical training as the county's chief medical authority on deaths, more questions surfaced about his investigation. The news media also wanted to know who had abducted Coach Geiger and why.

A few days later the FBI apprehended and arrested brothers, Jimmy and Jerry Smith in Egypt, Georgia. It would take them several days to find out who was responsible for one of the Lowcountry's most publicized abductions.

* * *

On the Friday before National Signing Day, Coach Hanover called Frankie into his office. He told Frankie about the details concerning the ceremony that we had planned in the school's gymnasium. He wanted to make sure that Frankie knew his family could attend. He then asked, "Have you made a decision?"

Frankie looked at Coach Hanover and replied, "Yes, sir, I have."

Coach Hanover paused for a few moments hoping that Frankie would reveal his choice. Once he realized that Frankie wasn't volunteering the information freely, he said, "You know that at all the fancy college signin' day ceremonies, a lot of the players put on the cap of the college they choose. It makes for a good picture."

"Coach Blake told me."

"I hate to do this to you, but if you want me to buy you the hats, I'll need to know which schools you're considerin'."

"Coach Blake has already taken care of it."

* * *

On Wednesday, February 5, 1986, at 8:30 am, students, staff, journalists, special guests, friends, family, and football enthusiasts gathered in the Coosawhatchie County High School Gymnasium to witness the biggest announcement in the history of the school. Coach Hanover and I were dressed in our best suits. We had been at the school setting up a long cafeteria table draped with a homemade construction banner made by the Coosawhatchie High

School cheerleaders. The banner simply read: CCHS in bold green letters.

Shah and Paige Hanover also arrived early so they could help. They were the ones who decided that it would be best to place the table on the edge of the gym's stage so that everyone could have a good view of the ceremony. Principal Dean helped me set up the school's microphone while *Lowcountry Times* sports editor, Gerald Davis guided other journalists as they set up numerous television cameras.

By the time Frankie, James, and Ida Louise Lake arrived, the student body was becoming loud. The Lake family was greeted by Frankie's best friend, Doug Pye who was wearing a pair of blue jeans, and a Virginia Tech football shirt. He whispered to Frankie, "I know everyone is here for you, but when Coach Blake said they wanted to honor me today, I couldn't pass up the chance to be with you when you signed."

Never in the history of the school had there been so many people packed into the gym during the school day for a non-athletic event. Coach Hanover and I took a moment and scanned across the gym. I had to yell at him to be heard. "What a Crowd!"

"Well, which college did Frankie pick?"

"I have no idea. I thought he told you."

"I guess we'll find out like the rest of the world because he damn sure didn't tell me."

Right before we started the ceremony, I opened a large brown paper sack and began placing college hats on the table. When I pulled out the first hat, several of the students, who were watching closely, began booing when they realized it was a Penn State hat. The media, noticing what was taking place, began focusing their attention on my hat revelations. The next hat I placed on the table received another very loud round of boos when everyone realized it was a University of Tennessee hat. While Frankie, his family, and Doug walked up onto the stage, I pulled out another hat.

Frankie and Doug laughed at how a Michigan hat set off the loudest boo of all. When I placed my hand back inside the brown paper sack, many of the students began banging on the bleachers making the sound of a drum roll. As I pulled out two hats at one time, the gymnasium erupted when they could clearly see both a Clemson University and a University of South Carolina hat. Their cheers and applause were so loud and deafening, nobody heard Coach Hanover when he first tried to speak into the microphone.

Finally, after everyone calmed down, he thanked everyone in attendance. He then introduced Doug Pye and the Lake family. Coach Hanover spoke briefly about their accomplishments as football players and students. Before he turned it over to me he said, "This is a special day for all of Coosawhatchie County."

I then told the audience that Doug Pye would be accepting a scholarship to Virginia Tech. The crowd clapped as Doug stood up from his chair and waved back to them. He then took out a Bic pen and pretended to sign his commitment papers while the news media took his photograph. While the photographs of Doug were being taken, some of the students began to chant, "We want Frankie. We want Frankie."

Principal Dean immediately took the microphone and said, "Y'all behave over there. Give Doug the respect he deserves."

Doug smiled and said to Frankie, "They better hurry up with these pictures 'cause these folks have come to see what you're gonna do."

I then announced that Frankie was about to choose which college or university he would be attending. The crowd went wild. Frankie was sitting in the middle chair behind the special table on the gym's stage. I took a few steps and handed him the microphone. Frankie waited for everyone to be quiet before he said in a soft voice, "I guess I'm supposed to do this now."

Many people began laughing. Frankie waited for them to quiet down. As an entire community anxiously awaited, Frankie slid his hand into his navy-blue blazer. He then shouted, "I have decided to stay in the state of South Carolina."

When he said those words, the crowd stood up and began cheering wildly. He waited for a few seconds more before looking at his buddy, Doug Pye. Then as the crowd began to settle back down, Frankie Lake stood up from his chair and pulled out the hat. He placed it on his head. It was a camouflage hat. Nobody who saw the hat could make out what college or university it was supposed to represent. The crowd began to chatter. One person from the news media quickly shouted, "Is that supposed to be an Army hat representing West Point?"

James Lake stood up, walked over behind his son, and took away the microphone from Frankie. "My son Frankie, has decided to join the Marines instead of going to college. He will be training at Parris Island right down the road from here."

While several people in the gym began clapping, others were furious. Henry Bozzard, who was standing in the very back of the gym, cried out, "What are you doing? Clemson wants you."

The mayor of Coosawhatchie, Gamecock Gene then yelled, "Don't you listen to him. The University of South Carolina has a place for you, son. Do the right thing for you and your family. Sign with Carolina."

The news media and many others began shouting questions at Frankie like he had committed a crime. Hanover and I immediately ushered Frankie and his family off the stage and into Hanover's office while Principal Dean and other school staff members tried to calm down the chaos that was happening in the gym. Two fights broke out in the stands as tensions were high among students who had placed bets on which school Frankie would select.

Inside the office, Coach Hanover looked at Frankie and asked, "What are you doing? Don't you realize that you're turning down a lot of money in this deal?"

“I’m only doin’ what you said was the most important thing in life.”

Coach Hanover looked at me. “I have no idea what he's talking ‘bout.”

“Coach, you were the one who told me this summer that the most important thing in life is service to others. You said service was more important than money or fame. I want to serve others, and I figured the best way I can serve is by bein’ a Marine. I want to be a Marine just like you.”

Hanover walked over to Frankie, put his arms around him and gave him a big hug. The veteran coach of many years became emotional. At first, he couldn’t say a word. He was so impressed not only by what Frankie said, but also by the way he said it. He could not believe how much better his diction and enunciation had become in such a short time. Then when he gathered his composure he said, “I didn’t mean to talk you out of money, but I want you to know that I support and respect your decision. I’m so proud of the young man that you have become.”

I became choked up and could barely say a word when I also gave Frankie a big hug. I said, “There is no doubt that you will be the most talked about man in the country. There is nobody as special as you, Frankie Lake.”

* * *

For the rest of the day Hanover and I fielded phone calls from all over the nation. Reporters from media outlets wanted quotes. College coaches who were disappointed wanted to find out if they could capitalize on the possibility that Frankie Lake was stressed or confused when he made his decision; hoping the young man may see the light. Coach Hanover and I were surprised by the anger that Frankie’s decision brought out in people who had no investment in Frankie’s future. People in town began to accuse others of hijacking Frankie Lake’s future. Some accused Coach Hanover of his undue influence while others pointed their fingers at me. Some in the community blamed Frankie's pastor Dr. Osborne, and others jumped all over a rumor that the ROTC instructor at the school had influenced Frankie when it was revealed that he was the one, who introduced Frankie to a Marine recruiter from Charleston.

That afternoon, I received a phone call from Coach Danny Ford at Clemson. I reluctantly took the phone call thinking that Coach Ford might voice his displeasure to what had occurred. Instead, he said, "I heard you had some fireworks go off down there this morning." He laughed for a moment and then continued by saying, "I don't mind tellin' you that Coach Aldridge and myself were shocked when we heard the news. I'm pretty sure everyone down there was just as shocked."

"You can say that again, Coach."

"Well, you win some and you lose some. Just between you and me, I'm so glad he didn't sign with you know who. I'm also sure that you and Coach B. B. did what you could do to advise Frankie about his future. I just wanted to let you know that I have really enjoyed getting to know you. If you're ever up in my neck of the woods you make sure to come by and visit with us. I'll definitely be in touch."

Not long after I hung up with Coach Ford, Coach Fulmer from the University of Tennessee called. He said, "I have been doing this for a while, and I don't think I have ever heard of such. I'm sure that you guys were as stunned as we were."

"How did Coach Majors take the news?"

"Oh, he took it all in stride. In this business the only thing you can do is move on. In a few months we'll be parked somewhere else trying to sign the next Frankie Lake. I can tell you right now, that we'll be back down there in a few months. I really like the way that Mazyck kid moves. I have a feeling he will become a big-time recruit." He paused for a moment and then continued by saying, "I want you to know that I enjoyed my time down there at your school. It's a little too humid for my liking, but if I can ever help you in any way, please do not hesitate to give me a call."

A few minutes later, Coach Kenney called me and said, "Coach Paterno laughed and told all of our coaches at Penn State that Frankie had forever changed the landscape of college recruiting."

"How is that?"

"He told us that we now had to out-recruit the military recruiters. Coach Paterno said to let you know that we'll be back down there next year. We obviously want the Mazyck kid like everyone else, but I'm here to tell you that I have my eyes on that Jacobs kid. He is one hell of a linebacker."

A few minutes later, Coach Treadway from Virginia Tech called. "I heard the news. I bet you guys are busy trying to figure it all out. I want you to know that I'll be thinking about you as the media circus comes your way. If you ever need anything- call me."

* * *

Frankie's decision not to attend college made national news when the CBS show, *60 Minutes* ran a story a week later about a poor disadvantaged teenager in South Carolina, who gave up fortune to serve in the military. In the same episode, they ran a story about Coach Jaden Geiger's abduction and miraculous escape from Egypt, Georgia. Those stories definitely put Coosawhatchie County on the national map.

The *60 Minutes* episodes about two South Carolina feel-good stories led to fame and fortune for both young men as they both appeared on national talk shows and were written about in national publications.

Coach Geiger never coached again. His television appearances led to a lucrative contract where he became a fixture at ESPN as a college football analyst for more than three decades. During his time working at ESPN, he never mentioned the kidnapping again.

Frankie Lake went through boot camp at Parris Island that summer. However, his boot camp was far different from every other Marine who spent time at the notoriously tough camp. Frankie spent three months of intensive training to become the voice and face of National Marine Recruitment. After attending speech therapy classes, Frankie Lake became one polished spokesperson. His story along with his positive attitude served the Marine Corp well, as he eventually traveled across the nation making a career spreading the gospel about service in the military.

One year after Frankie turned down college football, Henry Bozzard publicly delivered a ten thousand dollar check to Frankie Lake. Frankie immediately turned over the money to the Coosawhatchie County Parks and Recreation Department to renovate the same football field where he first played ball. To this day, everyone in Coosawhatchie County knows where the Frankie Lake Recreational Field is located.

As the winds of March rolled into Coosawhatchie County that year, the FBI held a press conference at the Federal Building in downtown Columbia, South Carolina to reveal that they had issued an arrest warrant for Donald Chafin, known as Tiger Don. Indicted for the abduction and kidnapping of Coach Jaden Geiger, Tiger Don and his young bride fled South Carolina long before authorities could make an arrest. When it was later revealed that the misguided Tiger Don arranged for the abduction of Coach Geiger in an attempt to hinder the University of South Carolina from signing Frankie Lake to a football scholarship, Tiger Don became the most hated person in Coosawhatchie County. A few weeks after the announcement, the South Carolina Highway Department repaved the highway in front of his house and erased the tiger paw logos forever. Three months later, his orange mansion mysteriously went up in flames and burned to the ground.

While the FBI conducted a nationwide manhunt for Tiger Don, attorneys with the NCAA worked side- by- side with the Coosawhatchie Solicitor, Luke McRoy to find out if Coach Danny

Ford and Clemson University played a role in Coach Geiger's abduction. During the trial of the Smith brothers, Jimmy and Jerry both testified that they believed that Tiger Don was the lone instigator. Covering the sensational trial of the Smith Brothers, Chris Berman of ESPN made the famous announcement, "And they went All...The... Way. Two blundering criminal brothers in Egypt clear the name of Coach Danny Ford."

* * *

Two months after Frankie's famous announcement, Shah and I were once again walking into a room at the Savannah Christian Hospital. This time Frankie was with us. Before we entered the room, we all knew that a day earlier, Coach Hanover had driven himself to the hospital after experiencing chest pains. Against his doctor's advice, he overdid it on a humid spring day while cutting some shrubbery and hauling away some limbs from his backyard. He didn't suffer another heart attack but his blood pressure was extremely high. It was so high, the cardiologist told Paige that if he didn't follow orders and rest, he would be gone sooner than later.

The first thing we noticed as we entered the hospital room were the many cards and flowers from family, friends, local boosters, and college football coaches. Paige read a card attached to a large peace lily wrapped in garnet and black bows. It read: "Get well soon... Coach Joe Morrison... The University of South Carolina."

I walked over to the room's window ledge before bending over to smell a vase filled with two white roses. I looked at Paige and said, "I'm not much of a flower guy, but these are gorgeous. Who sent these?"

"The congregation of the Jerusalem Fire Baptized Church."

Coach Hanover said, "My own church didn't send flowers. Ain't that a heck of a note?"

Frankie picked up an orange Tennessee card sitting on the counter next to the sink. It was from Coach Johnny Majors. Frankie started laughing as he read the card.

Shah said, "What's so funny?"

Frankie looked at me before replying, "Coach knows why... It has something to do with a grapefruit and the Volunteers."

Shah pointed at a garden basket filled with white geraniums. She said, "Joe Paterno from Penn State sent those.'

I walked over to the hospital window ledge and looked at the card. It read: "Thinking of you, Coach B.B."

I then walked over to Hanover and whispered to him, "You're one lucky man. Look at all the people who care about you. People from all over the country love you."

"You're pretty lucky yourself. A year ago, I bet you never dreamed that you would be standing here as a state championship coach, married, with a child on the way." Then with a sentimental reply he pulled me closer to him and whispered, "I don't know how long I have, but I want you to know how proud I am of the man you have become. Somehow, I think my friend, Donte' Davis of Willacoochee, Georgia is smiling right now. Always remember to let the boys know that we all 'bleed green' at Coosawhatchie."

Paige heard what he said. She then turned toward Shah with a small tear in her eye. She quickly began laughing to hide her emotions before saying, "I haven't had time to call you and congratulate you on the good news."

Frankie walked around the hospital bed and gave Shah a big hug before saying, "Whenever I'm home, you always have a babysitter. Mama said y'all can always bring the baby to our house. She said y'all better bring it by once it's born so she can see it."

I said, "I couldn't imagine anything could ever be more special than winning a football championship. I can already tell that being a father will be more special."

Hanover said, "You're right about that. Being a parent is the most special thing a person can experience on this earth." He then looked over at Frankie and continued. "You will be up to bat before you know it. I bet there will be a lot of little Lake kids running around your parent's place one day."

"Coach, I have to find a wife before I start thinking that way."

Shah said, "You promise that whenever that day comes, we are invited to the wedding."

Coach Hanover leaned up in his hospital bed and said, "Frankie findin' a girlfriend will be a miracle much less him findin' a wife."

"Don't listen to him," Paige said. "Frankie. Some girl will be lucky to land you as a husband one day."

After a lot of small talk about the weather and the upcoming football season, we listened and were entertained as Coach Hanover told a few stories about his old days of coaching. After he finished, I asked Frankie, "During your college football recruitment we all had our ideas about which college you were going to choose. Just out of curiosity, which one of the schools would you have picked if you had decided to attend college?"

Frankie looked all around the room at everyone. He kept them waiting a while before saying in a most dignified tone of voice, "I like them all."

Made in United States
Orlando, FL
25 May 2024